Technology Projects

for
4–7 year olds

Rebecca Green

Brilliant Publications

Publisher's information

Brilliant Publications
1 Church View
Sparrow Hall Farm
Edlesborough
Dunstable
Bedfordshire LU6 2ES

Tel: 01525 229720
Fax: 01525 229725

e-mail: sales@brilliantpublications.co.uk
website: www.brilliantpublications.co.uk

Written by Rebecca Green
Illustrated by Geraldine Sloane, with additional illustrations by Lynda Murray
Cover illustrated by Lynda Murray

© User Friendly Resource Enterprises Ltd.
Originally published in New Zealand, August 2001
User Friendly Resource Enterprises Ltd.

First published in the UK 2004
ISBN number: 1 903853 52 4
10 9 8 7 6 5 4 3 2 1

The right of Rebecca Green to be identified as the author of this work has been asserted by her in accordance with the Copyright, Design and Patents Act 1988.

All rights reserved. Pages 9–91 may be photocopied for use by the purchasing institution only. No other part of this publication may be reproduced, stored in a retrieval system, or transmitted in any form, or by any means electronic, mechanical, photocopying, recording or otherwise, without prior permission from the publisher.

Printed in Malta by Interprint Limited.

Contents

Introduction	5
Rain hats	6–17
Integrating other curriculum areas	6
Project overview	7
Suggested lesson sequence	8
Group the hats	9–10
How are hats different?	11
Are these good rain hats?	12
What could you use?	13
How waterproof should it be?	14
My rain hat designs	15
My absorbency test	16
Testing my hat	17
That's rubbish!	18–29
Integrating other curriculum areas	18
Project overview	19
Suggested lesson sequence	20
School litter survey	21
Graph of what's in our rubbish bin	22
What happens to our rubbish?	23
What can we recycle?	24
What do we know about composts?	25
What do we need to make a compost bin?	26
My compost bin designs	27
Advertising our bins	28
Testing my bin	29
The treasure boat	30–39
Integrating other curriculum areas	30
Project overview	31
Suggested lesson sequence	32
Naming the parts	33
Different kinds of floating craft	34
How do we use boats?	35
What floats and what sinks?	36
Make a paper treasure boat!	37
Planning our treasure boats	38
Testing my treasure boat	39
Paper making	40–49
Integrating other curriculum areas	40
Project overview	41
Suggested lesson sequence	42
How do we use paper?	43
Paper for paper making!	44
Paper making equipment	45
Making paper	46
Different types of paper	47
Colour the paper	48
Can you make paper?	49

© User Friendly Resource Enterprises Ltd.

Brilliant Publications
www.brilliantpublications.co.uk

Contents

You've got mail! 50–59
Integrating other curriculum areas 50
Project overview 51
Suggested lesson sequence 52
What happens when we post a letter? 53
Writing a letter 54
Stamps 55
Design a stamp 56
Envelopes 57
Classroom post 58
Design a post box 59
Testing our postal system 60

The picnic party 61–70
Integrating other curriculum areas 61
Project overview 62
Suggested lesson sequence 63
What will we take on our picnic? 64
Graph of our favourite sandwiches 65
What will happen to unprotected food? 66
How are food containers different? 67
How do we store different foods? 68
Designing our picnic containers 69
Testing my container 70

Let's go fly a kite! 71–80
Integrating other curriculum areas 71
Project overview 72
Suggested lesson sequence 73
What is a kite? 74
What is symmetry? 75
Making a parachute 76
Kites from other cultures 77
What material will be best for my kite? 78
Making our kites: teacher information 79
Flying our kites 80
Testing my kite 81

Teddy chairs 82–91
Integrating other curriculum areas 82
Project overview 83
Suggested lesson sequence 84
Chairs and people 85
Making a tower 86
What makes a chair strong? 87
What makes a chair safe? 88
How have chairs changed? 89
Making our designs 90
Testing my teddy chair 91

Introduction

Technology is a fun and hands-on subject to teach all children. This resource book contains eight complete technology projects suitable for children in reception classes and Key Stage 1 (4–7 year olds). The projects integrate easily with other areas of the curriculum. Each project starts with an overview page which gives details of the major technology focus.

Project	Technology focus	Context
Rain hats	Materials technology	Personal
That's rubbish!	Biotechnology	School, environmental
The treasure boat	Materials technology	Recreational, business
Paper making	Production and process	Industrial, home
You've got mail!	ICT	Personal, school
The picnic party	Food technology	Home, recreational
Let's go fly a kite!	Materials technology	Recreational
Teddy chairs	Structures and mechanisms	Home, school

The project structure
Each project contains a design brief for children to work towards. The work is structured so that children gain some background understanding of the topic in the first half of the project. This is important for young children. Once the children have some understanding of the topic, lessons covering the design process are introduced. Evaluating lessons are included at the end of each project.

Young children and technology
Organising a class full of 4–7 year old children to design, make and evaluate a project can be a little daunting! The projects can be adapted by enlarging worksheets to A3 size and completing as a whole class or group activity. Parents or helpers are invaluable for enabling children to work one-on-one on their projects. The making and evaluating could be done individually, in groups or as a whole class, depending on the needs of the children.

Rain hats | **Integrating other curriculum areas**

Rain hats

Science
Materials
Water
Fair test
Fabric and fibre
Insulation
Waterproofing

English
Following instructions
Rain poems

Mathematics
Shapes
Measuring circumference

Geography
Hats from other cultures
Hats and occupations

Art and design
Hat design
Fabric and fibre construction

Physical education
Hats used in sports

PSHE
Safety
Caring for ourselves

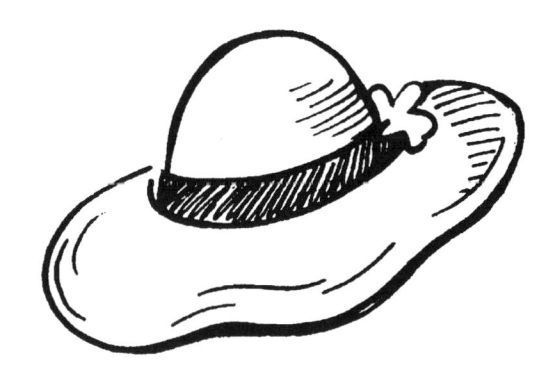

Project overview

Rain hats

Hats and technology

A study of hats is a fun, hands-on project for children.
All children have some experience and background understanding of hats. As a way of beginning the project, children could bring some unusual hats from home. A fun way to develop the children's background understanding is to use drama to role play different ways that we use hats, 'Guess what this hat is for!'

In this project the children will focus on materials technology as they describe and test the features of different materials in order to select the best options for their hats. These activities also integrate well with science objectives.

With some support children are easily able to construct their own hats from a paper ring measured to fit around their heads. The area of structures and mechanisms could be covered by comparing other methods of constructing hats such as paper folding, and by testing strength.

Children could be asked to help design a fair test to measure how strong and waterproof their hats are. During the project the children will use the design process to plan, make and evaluate their own rain hats.

This project can be adapted for younger children by enlarging worksheets to A3 size and completing as a whole class activity.

Extension ideas

- Follow instructions to fold paper hats. Can pupils adapt the design?
- Investigate hats from other cultures or times.
- Visit a hat shop or invite a milliner to demonstrate hat making to the class.
- Write stories about wearing a magical hat.
- Read out an extract from the Harry Potter series about the Sorting Hat!
- Plan a hat parade to show off the pupils' creations.

Assessment

Each of the activity sheets represents an objective outlined on the lesson sequence page. Photocopies of the completed template sheets can be used as samples for the purpose of portfolio assessment, or included in the cumulative files of each child.

Suggested lesson sequence

Rain hats

Design brief
We all know what a baseball cap looks like. Let's see if we can design a hat to keep us dry in the rain!

Lesson 1: Setting the scene
Key question: How do people use hats?
Learning objective: The pupils will group a variety of hats under the headings; safety hats, fun hats and work hats.
Template: Group the hats

Lesson 2: Developing background knowledge
Key questions: How are hats different? Why are hats different?
Learning objective: The pupils will complete a chart to show the different features of a good rain hat.
Templates: How are hats different? Are these good rain hats?

Lesson 3: Considering the options
Key questions: What type of materials are used in making hats? Why are these materials used?
Learning objective: The pupils will complete a chart to describe the features of different types of material.
Template: What could you use?

Lesson 4: Defining the problem
Key question: What kind of hat and material would protect us in the rain?
Learning objective: The pupils will brainstorm the type of features a good rain hat would have.
Template: How waterproof should it be?

Lesson 5: Deciding on a solution
Key question: What will rain hats look like?
Learning objective: The pupils will draw their plans of rain hats.
Template: My rain hat designs

Lesson 6: Constructing our designs
Key question: What's the best material for our designs?
Learning objective: The pupils will test three material samples to discover which is the most water resistant.
Template: My absorbency test

Lesson 7: Presenting and testing our designs
Key questions: How did I make this hat? Why did I make this hat?
Learning objective: The pupils will share their designs and test the protection they offer.

Lesson 8: Evaluating our designs
Key questions: What were the good parts of my hat? What needs improvement?
Learning objective: The pupils will reflect on the performance of their hats.
Template: Testing my hat

Group the hats

Rain hats

Group the hats by pasting them on the heads below.

Fun hats

Work hats

Safety hats

© User Friendly Resource Enterprises Ltd.

Brilliant Publications
www.brilliantpublications.co.uk

Rain hats

Group the hats

Cut the hats out along the dotted lines and paste them into the correct boxes.

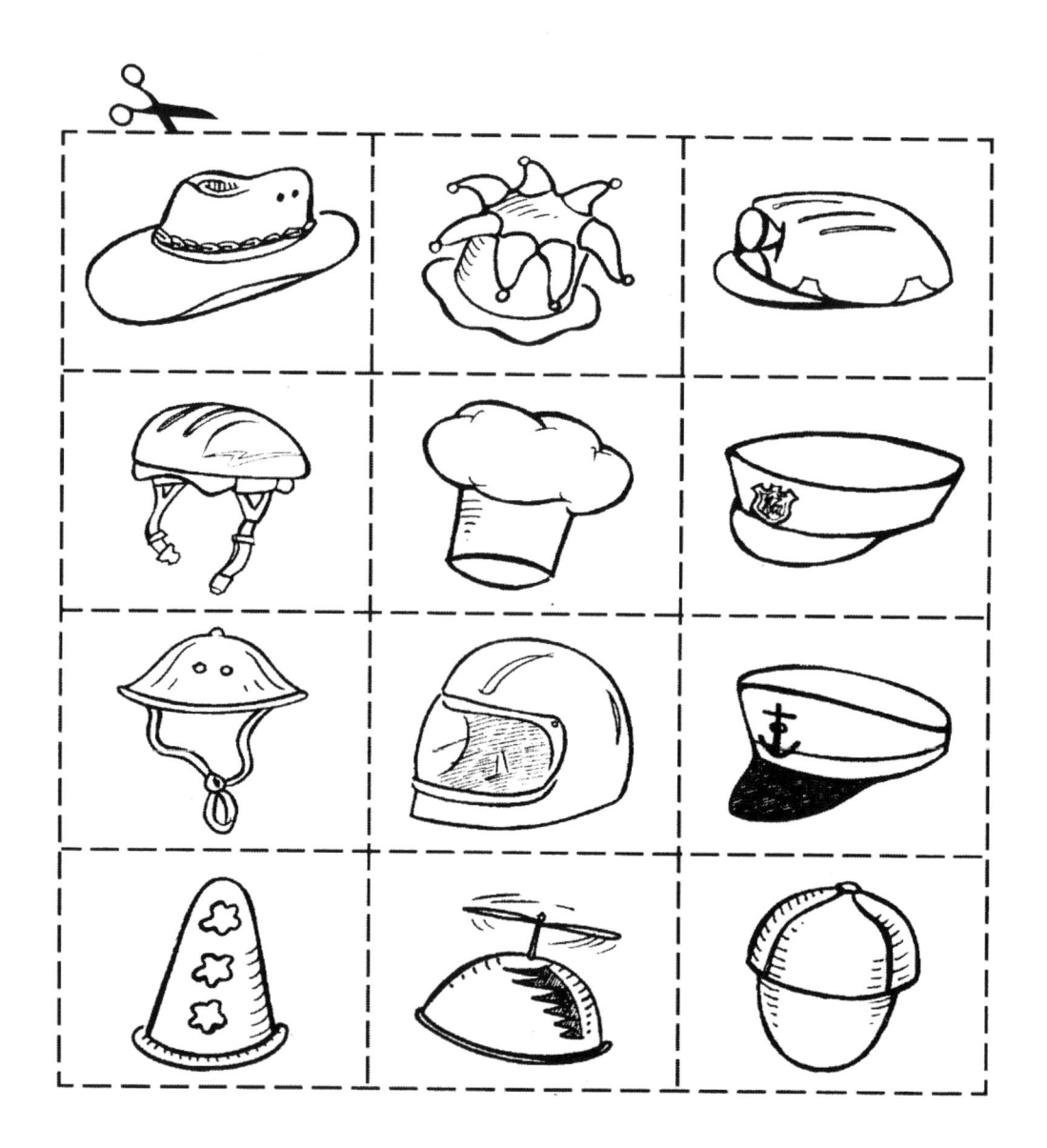

Note to teachers: Enlarge pages 9 and 10 by the same percentage to make the hats fit the boxes.

How are hats different?

Rain hats

The hat	What is it made of?	What is special about it?	What is it used for?

Brilliant Publications
www.brilliantpublications.co.uk

© User Friendly Resource Enterprises Ltd.

11

Rain Hats

Are these good rain hats?

Draw a hat that would be good for the rain!

What could you use?

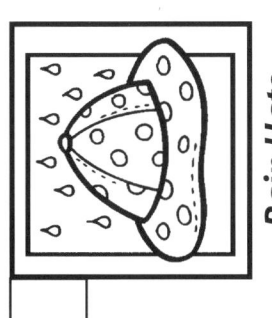

Rain Hats

Colour the pictures to describe your fabric.	Is it strong?	Is it light?	Does it look good?	Is it warm?	Is it waterproof?	Draw a hat that you could make with this fabric
Glue the fabric						
Glue the fabric						
Glue the fabric						

© User Friendly Resource Enterprises Ltd.

Rain Hats

How waterproof should it be?

What is it like to be out in the rain?

Write your ideas in the raindrops.

A rain hat should have ...

_____
_____
_____
_____
_____

My rain hat designs

Rain Hats

How can you make it strong, waterproof and still look good? Draw your ideas in the rain clouds.

1

2

3

4

Is your fabric waterproof? When you've tested it – make a hat!

© User Friendly Resource Enterprises Ltd.

Brilliant Publications
www.brilliantpublications.co.uk

Rain hats

My absorbency test

1. You will need a straw, a cup, some water, sticky tape, a pen, a watch, a ruler and three pieces of fabric.

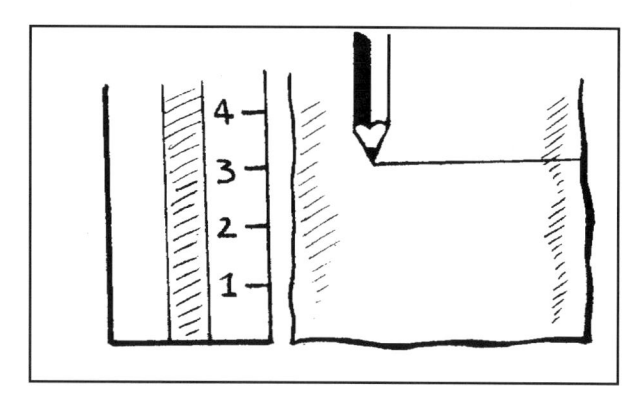

2. Draw a line along the fabric that is three centimetres from the bottom.

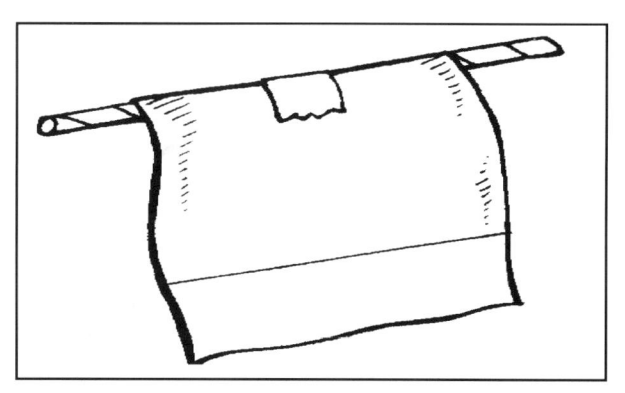

3. Tape the fabric to the straw.

4. Put the straw on top of the cup.

5. Fill the cup with water so that the fabric is just touching the top of the water.

6. Record the time it takes for the water to reach the mark.

1. _____
2. _____
3. _____

Testing my hat

Rain hats

Name_____

Is my hat waterproof?	☺ ☐ ☹
Does my hat look good?	☺ ☐ ☹
Is my hat strong?	☺ ☐ ☹

The best part of my hat is ...

Next time I could ...

Integrating other curriculum areas

That's rubbish!

Science
Decomposing
Sorting rubbish
Gardens

English
Advertising
Symbols

Mathematics
Graphing types of litter

Geography
Caring for the environment
Where does our rubbish go?

Art and design
Construction using recycled materials

PSHE
Effects of pollution on health

Project overview

That's rubbish!

Rubbish and technology

Rubbish is a popular area of study in key stage classrooms. This technology project can easily be integrated with science and geography-based work.

The project can be adapted for younger children by enlarging templates to A3 size and completing as a whole class activity. It may also be easier to design and make one compost system for the whole class to promote and use.

The focus for this project is biotechnology, the use of organisms to benefit the environment. It is a good project for investigating the way that technology can assist people in caring for the environment. The project includes opportunities for the children to gather and graph data in a basic form.

Extension ideas

- Make a 'rubbish monster' out of household rubbish to share at school.
- Design other ways to reuse rubbish.
- Investigate how long different food groups take to decompose.
- Find out what happens to the school rubbish once it is collected.
- Visit a rubbish dump or recycling centre.
- Make a class garden to use the compost that has been made.

Assessment

Each of the activity sheets represents a learning objective outlined on the lesson sequence page. Photocopies of the completed template sheets can be used as samples for the purpose of portfolio assessment, or included in the cumulative files of each child.

That's rubbish!

Suggested lesson sequence

> **Design brief**
> What can we do with all those food scraps from our classroom?

Lesson 1: Setting the scene
Key questions: Where can we find litter in our school?
What is in our rubbish?
Learning objective: The pupils will complete a litter walk around the school. The pupils will investigate and categorise the rubbish for a week.
Templates: School litter survey
Graph of what's in our rubbish bin

Lesson 2: Developing background knowledge
Key question: What happens to our rubbish?
Learning objective: The pupils will complete a flow chart to show what happens to rubbish.
Template: What happens to our rubbish?

Lesson 3: Considering the options
Key question: What can we recycle?
Learning objective: The pupils will sort the pictures to show how we can recycle our rubbish.
Template: What can we recycle?

Lesson 4: Defining the problem
Key question: How can we recycle our food scraps?
Learning objective: The pupils will interview an expert on compost (such as the caretaker or a gardener), to understand the compost process.
Template: What do we know about composts?

Lesson 5: Deciding on a solution
Key question: What do we need to make a class compost bin?
Learning objective: The pupils will plan what equipment and resources they will need to collect the food scraps, to compost the scraps and to use the compost.
Template: What does a compost bin need?

Lesson 6: Constructing our designs
Key question: What will our compost system look like?
Learning objective: The pupils will draw their plans. Depending on the children's age the class could then make models of the compost bin, make a compost system together as a class or make individual compost systems.
Template: My compost bin designs

Lesson 7: Presenting and testing our designs
Key question: How can we encourage others to put their scraps in our compost?
Learning objective: The children will brainstorm ways of advertising their designs.
Template: Advertising our bins

Lesson 8: Evaluating our designs
Key question: Did the compost system reduce rubbish in our classroom?
Learning objective: The pupils will reflect on the performance of their system.
Template: Testing my bin

School litter survey

That's rubbish!

Go on a litter hunt around your school. Write or draw what you find in each area, inside or around the appropriate shape.

In the classroom ...

In the lunch area ...

Around our bags ...

In the gardens ...

In the playground ...

Graph of what's in our rubbish bin

That's rubbish!

Date: From _____ to _____

Tally chart

Record the data here ...

Food _____

Packaging _____

Paper _____

Other _____

Number of Items

10, 9, 8, 7, 6, 5, 4, 3, 2, 1

Food — Packaging — Paper — Other

Types of rubbish

Extra for experts

Make a comparison graph to show how much rubbish in our bin can be recycled.

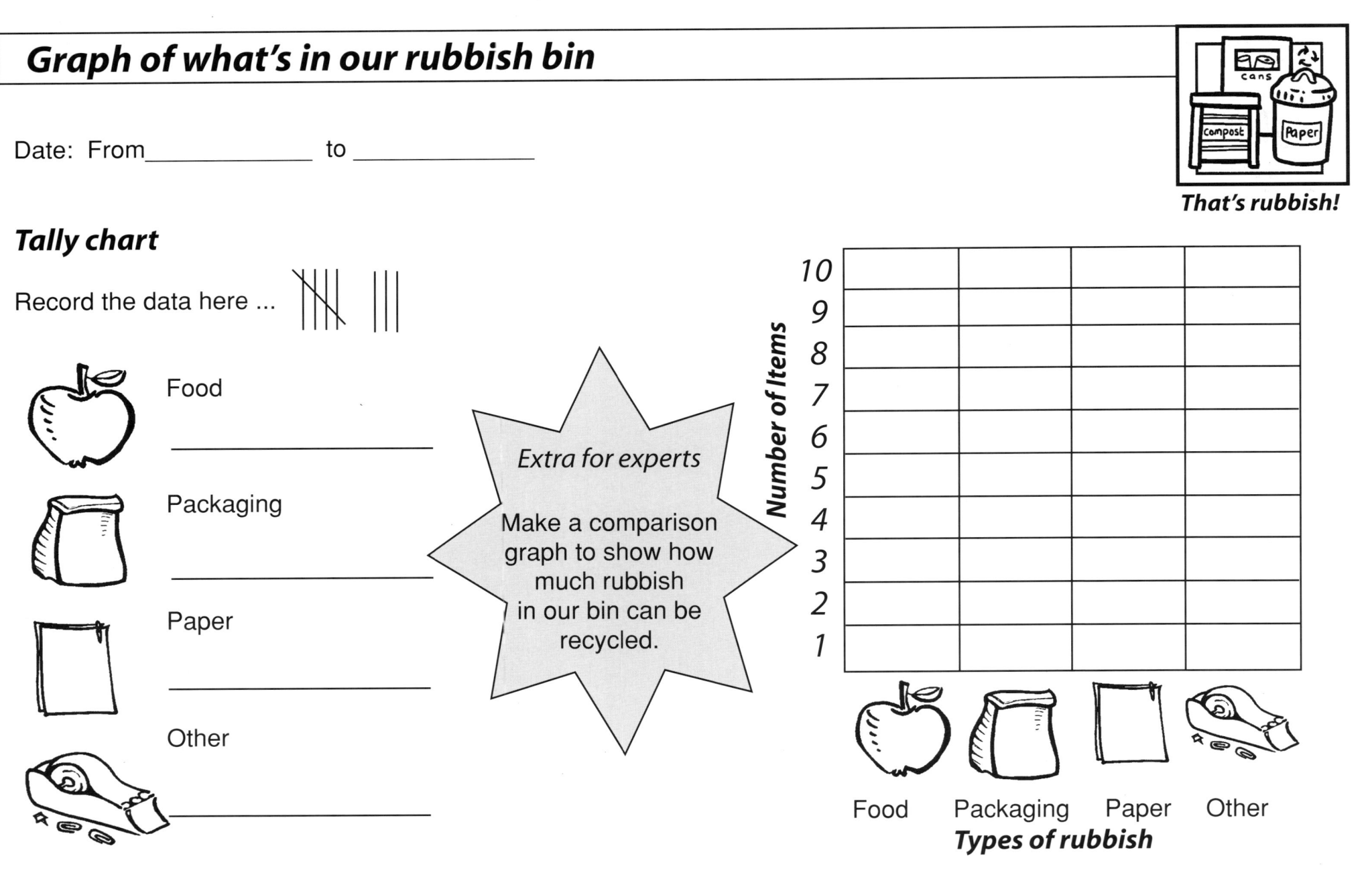

22 Brilliant Publications
www.brilliantpublications.co.uk

© User Friendly Resource Enterprises Ltd.

What happens to our rubbish?

That's rubbish!

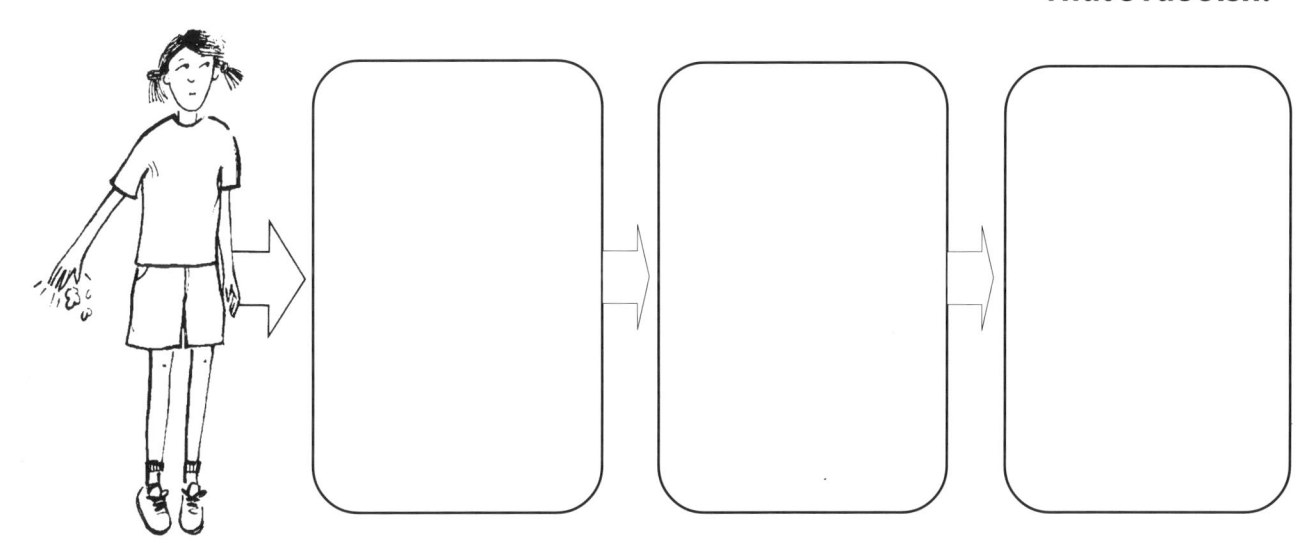

Write a story here about what you think happens to our rubbish.

_____
_____
_____
_____
_____

Paste some of these pictures in the boxes at the top of the page to show what might happen to our rubbish.

Brilliant Publications
www.brilliantpublications.co.uk

© User Friendly Resource Enterprises Ltd.

23

That's rubbish!

What can we recycle?

Sort the pictures and paste them onto the chart.

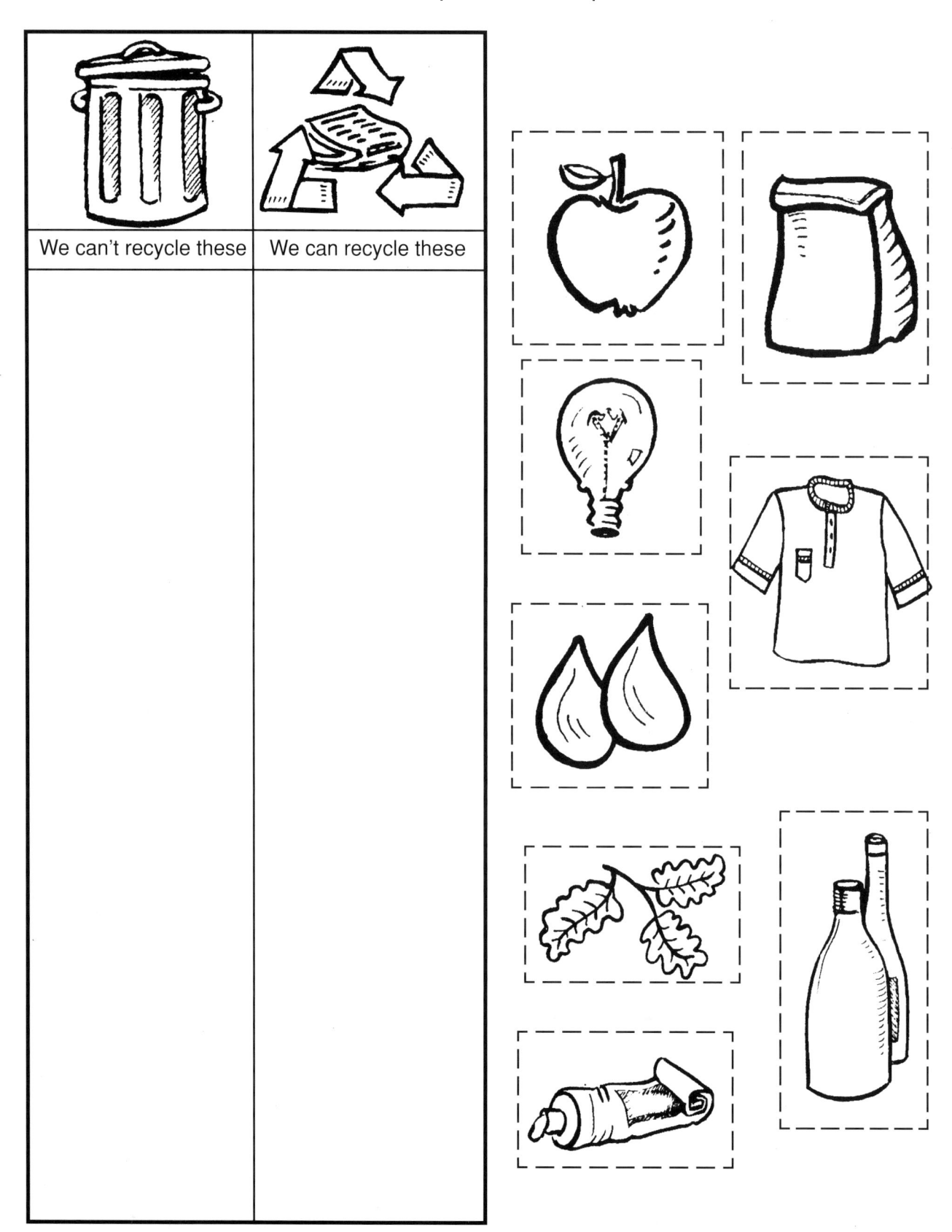

We can't recycle these	We can recycle these

24 **Brilliant Publications**
www.brilliantpublications.co.uk

© User Friendly Resource Enterprises Ltd.

What do we know about composts?

That's rubbish!

What is a compost heap?

What can you put in it?

Interview an expert to find out the facts!

When is it ready to use?

What can you use the compost for?

What does a compost bin need?

That's rubbish!

How will you collect the food scraps?

How will you get the finished compost out of the bin?

How will you make use of the compost?

What extras can you add to make your compost design amazing?

26   **Brilliant Publications**
www.brilliantpublications.co.uk   © *User Friendly Resource Enterprises Ltd.*

My compost bin designs

That's rubbish!

Draw your ideas, then choose your best one.

The materials I will need to make my best compost bin are:

_____   _____
_____   _____
_____   _____
_____   _____

That's rubbish!

Advertising our bins

How can we let everyone know about compost bins so that they will use them?

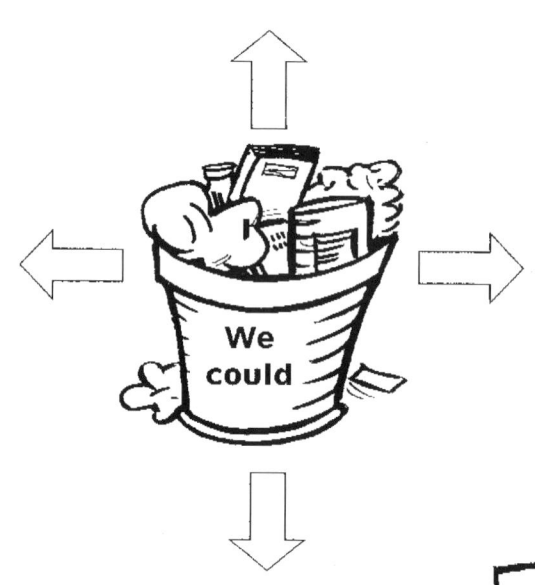

We could

Now make your own advertisement for the compost bin.

Don't forget ...

Have you told people what they can and can't put in the bin?

Is your advertisement bright and eye catching?

Where are you going to put your advertisement?

Testing my bin

That's rubbish!

Name _____

Have people used my bin?

☺ 😐 ☹

Does my bin look good?

☺ 😐 ☹

Has the compost been useful?

☺ 😐 ☹

The best part of my bin is ...

Next time I could ...

Brilliant Publications
www.brilliantpublications.co.uk

29

Integrating other curriculum areas

The treasure boat

Science
Floating and sinking
Materials
Fair testing

English
Instructions
Boating vocabulary
Sea poems, myths and legends

Mathematics
Measurement
Shapes
Counting

Geography
Boats from other cultures
Occupations using boats
Treasure chests

Art and design
Paper folding
Sea shanties and hornpipes
Pirate flags

Physical education
Boating sports
Water safety
Swimming

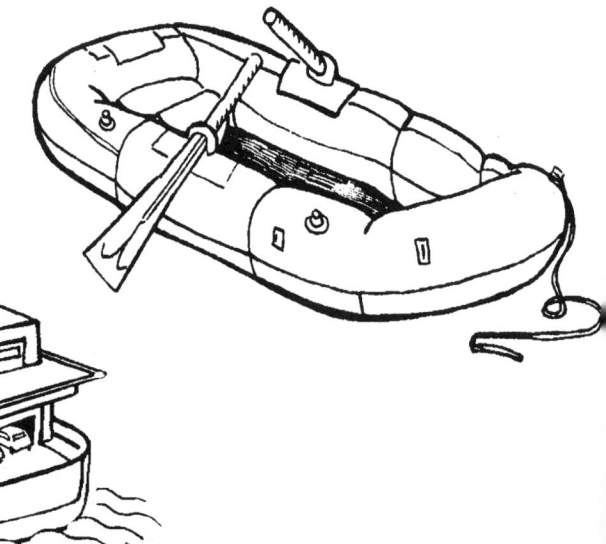

Project overview

The treasure boat

Boats and technology

Boats are so much fun to investigate with 5–7 year olds.
This project fits nicely with work on floating and sinking in science. There are additional links with health and physical education projects on water safety. The fantasy element also provides an opportunity to read sea myths and legends, talk about sunken treasure, and even invent a treasure island.

This project can be adapted for younger children by enlarging worksheets to A3 size and completing as a whole class activity.

The focus for this project is materials technology, as the children investigate which materials can float and are waterproof. The children also complete a fair test of their boats and this can be recorded as part of the assessment.

Extension ideas

- Visit a boat-building workshop.
- Investigate other helpful things that float such as life rings.
- Design a boat with a sail and have a race.
- Find out what ballast is.
- Experiment with an inflatable boat in the swimming pool.

Assessment

Each of the activity sheets represents a learning objective outlined on the lesson sequence page. Photocopies of the completed template sheets can be used as samples for the purpose of portfolio assessment, or included in the cumulative files of each child.

The treasure boat

Suggested lesson sequence

Design brief
How strong does a boat that carries treasure need to be?

Lesson 1: Setting the scene
Key question: What parts make up a boat?
Learning objective: The pupils will label the parts of a boat.
Template: Naming the parts

Lesson 2: Developing background knowledge
Key question: How are boats different?
Learning objective: The pupils will match labels to the correct boats.
Template: Different kinds of floating craft

Lesson 3: Considering the options
Key question: How do we use boats?
Learning objective: The pupils will identify different uses for boats.
Template: How do we use boats?

Lesson 4: Defining the problem
Key question: What is floating?
Learning objective: The pupils will investigate which objects float and which sink.
Template: What floats and what sinks?

Lesson 5: Deciding on a solution
Key question: How can we make a boat shape?
Learning objective: The children will make a paper boat.
Template: Make a paper treasure boat!

Lesson 6: Constructing our designs
Key question: What will my treasure boat look like?
Learning objective: The pupils will plan and make their boat.
Template: Planning our treasure boats

Lesson 7: Presenting and testing our designs
Key question: Did my treasure float?
Learning objective: The pupils will reflect on their boat design.
Template: Testing my treasure boat

Naming the parts

The treasure boat

Label the picture with the words below.

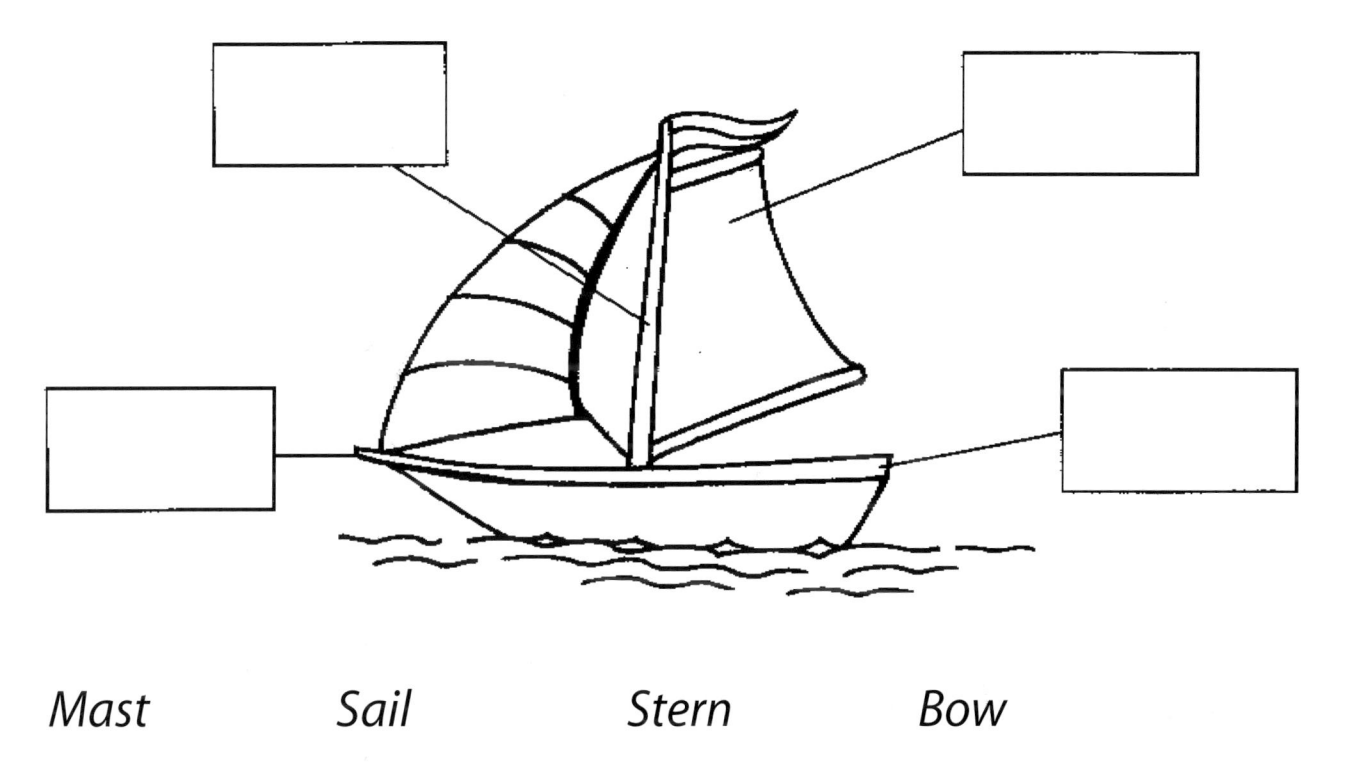

Mast   *Sail*   *Stern*   *Bow*

In the sail shape below draw all the things you might need on a boat.

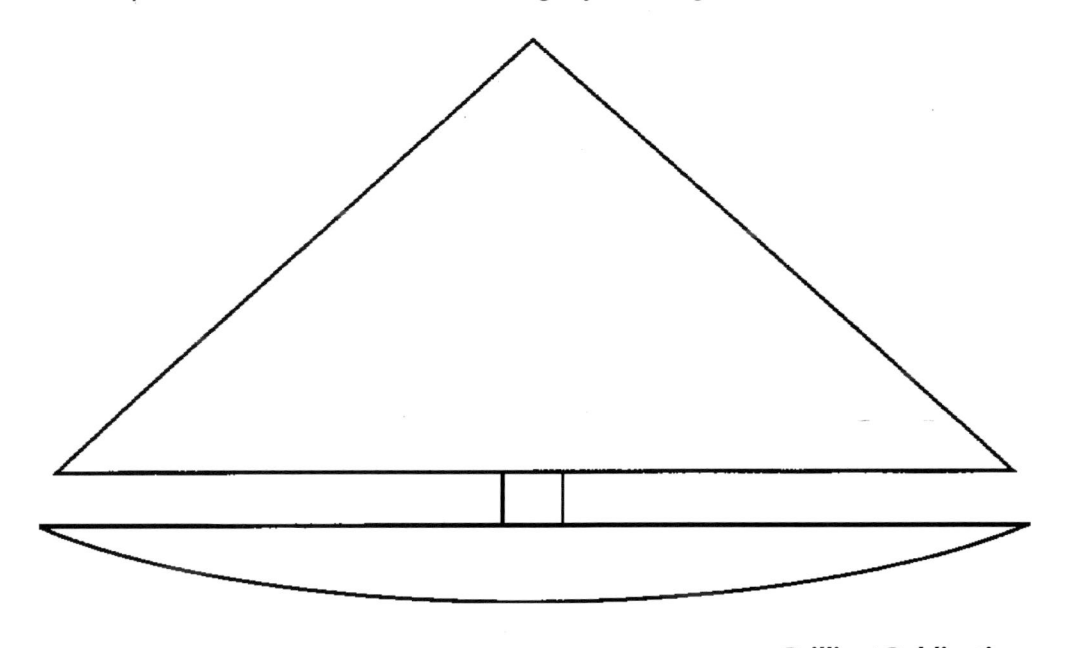

Brilliant Publications
www.brilliantpublications.co.uk

© User Friendly Resource Enterprises Ltd.

Different kinds of floating craft

The treasure boat

Match the labels to the pictures.

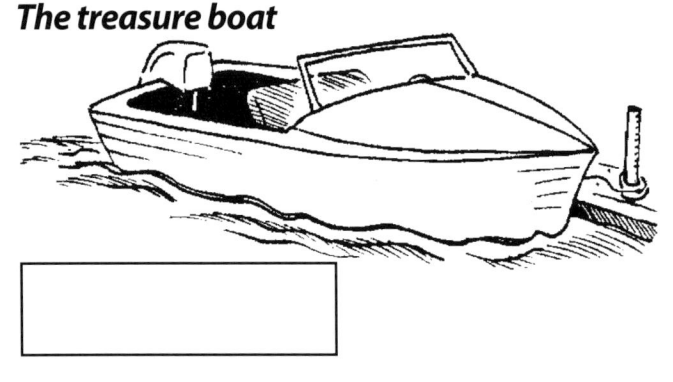

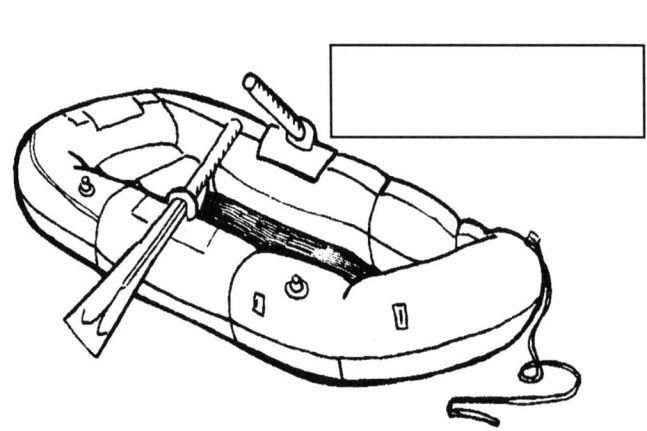

| Canoe | Ferry | Dinghy |
| Pirate Ship | Yacht | Speed boat |

34 Brilliant Publications
www.brilliantpublications.co.uk   © User Friendly Resource Enterprises Ltd.

How do we use boats?

The treasure boat

Sort these boats. Draw some of your own ideas too.

Boats for play	Boats for work

The treasure boat

What floats and what sinks?

Investigate what things float. Record your investigation by pasting pictures of the floating objects on top of the water and pictures of the sinking objects below the water.

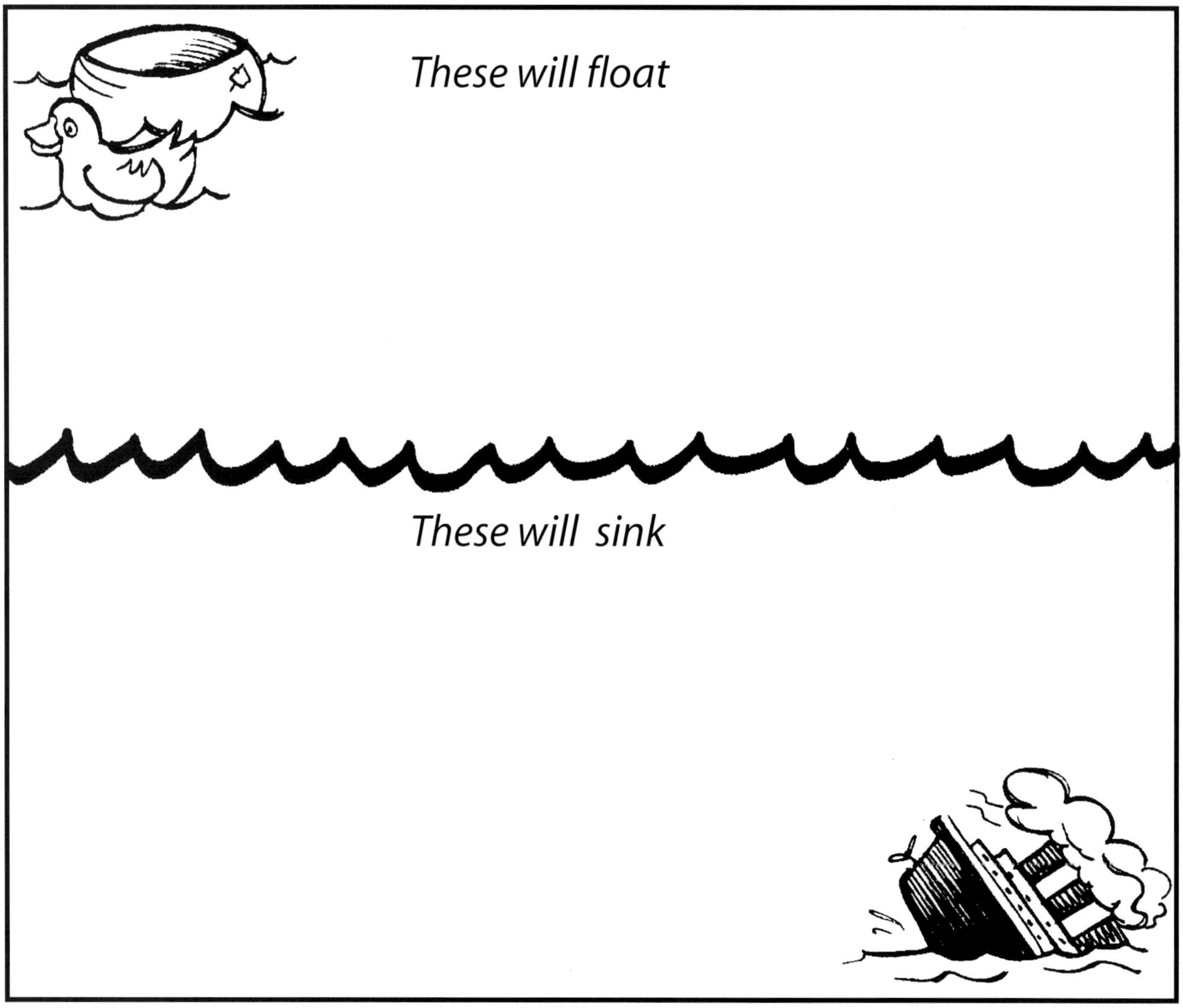

These will float

These will sink

Make a paper treasure boat!

The treasure boat

1. Start with a rectangular piece of paper like this:

2. Fold the paper top to bottom.

3. Now fold the paper right to left and unfold.

4. Fold the top corners into the middle fold.

5. Fold the top flap at the bottom up.

6. Turn the paper over and repeat.

7. It should now look like a pirate's hat.

8. Put your hands inside and pull out the front and back.

9. Squash the shape down into a diamond.

10. Fold the top flap at the bottom up.

11. Turn and repeat this step.

12. It should now look like a triangle.

13. Put your hands inside and pull out the front and back.

14. Squash the shape down into a diamond.

15. Lightly hold the top two triangles.

16. Pull them apart to shape your treasure boat. Colour it and make it sparkle.

© User Friendly Resource Enterprises Ltd.

Brilliant Publications
www.brilliantpublications.co.uk

The treasure boat

Planning our treasure boats

Now you've made a paper boat, try to make another boat out of different materials.

Your task is to build a treasure boat that will float and hold as much treasure (coins) as possible.

Draw your plans below. Make up one or two and see if they will hold coins while afloat!

Test these materials in water and choose the best design for your treasure boat:

paper	cardboard	plastic
string	wood	metal
cotton	felt	bottle tops
Plasticine®	Lego	straws
sticky tape	ice-block	sticks

38 Brilliant Publications
www.brilliantpublications.co.uk   © User Friendly Resource Enterprises Ltd.

Testing my treasure boat

Name ─────────────────────────────

The treasure boat

Did your treasure boat float?	😊 😐 ☹
Colour in the number of coins that floated in your treasure boat.	

The best part of my treasure boat is ...

Next time I could ...

Brilliant Publications
www.brilliantpublications.co.uk

Integrating other curriculum areas

Paper making

Science
Materials made from plants

English
Instructions
Visual presentations

Mathematics
Shapes and measurement

Geography
Papyrus and vellum

Art and design
Paper crafts
Marbling effects

Project overview

Paper making

Paper and technology

Although this is an interesting project to take with the class, paper making is an art and it pays to practise before demonstrating in front of the children! Alternatively one capable parent-help could be trained on the basics and then they could withdraw children one-on-one throughout the day to make their paper. This project would also be a good one to take with the help of a student teacher.

The project describes one easy method of making paper. Lots of books offer other methods that would also be interesting to try. Instead of making a special frame for the project, embroidery frames can be used. Paper making can get a little messy so it is often useful to make your paper outside.

This project can be adapted for younger children by enlarging worksheets to A3 size and completing as a whole class activity.

The focus for this project is production and process, in particular the manufacture of paper.

Extension ideas

- Make a scented or textured paper.
- Size the paper.
- Combine the paper making process with a system to recycle the school's scrap paper.
- Design paper crafts to make from the finished paper.
- Investigate other types of paper making such as paper made from cotton or plants.

Assessment

Each of the activity sheets represents a learning objective outlined on the lesson sequence page. Photocopies of the completed template sheets can be used as samples for the purpose of portfolio assessment, or included in the cumulative files of each child.

Paper making

Suggested lesson sequence

Design brief
Design systems to modify the process of making paper.

Lesson 1: Setting the scene
Key question: How do we use paper?
Learning objective: The pupils will identify how different people use paper.
Template: How do we use paper?

Lesson 2: Developing background knowledge
Key question: What kind of paper can we recycle in our paper making?
Learning objective: The pupils will identify the best kind of paper for recycling.
Template: Paper for paper making!

Lesson 3: Developing background knowledge
Key question: What things will we need to make paper?
Learning objective: The children will label the equipment used in paper making.
Template: Paper making equipment

Lesson 4: Developing background knowledge
Key question: How can we make paper?
Learning objective: The pupils will follow instructions to make their own paper. It may be useful to enlarge the instructions and read through as a whole class activity.
Template: Making paper

Lesson 5: Defining the problem
Key question: How can we make the paper more interesting?
Learning objective: The children will investigate the features of different types of paper.
Template: Different types of paper

Lesson 6: Deciding on a solution
Key question: How can we make coloured paper?
Learning objective: The pupils will experiment with different options in the paper making process.
Template: Colouring the paper

Lesson 7: Evaluating our designs
Key question: Did I achieve the type of effect I wanted to?
Learning objective: The pupils will reflect on the changes they implemented.
Template: Can you make paper?

How do we use paper?

Paper making

Ask your teacher and three classmates.

I use it to ...

I use it to ...

I use it to ...

I use it to ...

What did they use to write on at school a hundred years ago?

How will you find out the answer to this question?

Paper for paper making!

Paper making

The best kind of paper to use for making recycled paper pulp is sheets that have not been heavily printed.

Find some small samples of good and bad paper and paste them onto the chart below.

Do use ...	Don't use ...
Tissues, computer paper, photocopying paper, brown paper or envelopes	Magazines, whole newspapers or paper which has been glued, taped or stapled.

N.B. Newspapers and magazines can be used if they are boiled in detergent to remove all of the ink.

Paper making equipment

Paper making

Match the equipment with the labels.
Cut along the dotted lines, and on a separate piece of paper paste the correct name under each piece of equipment.

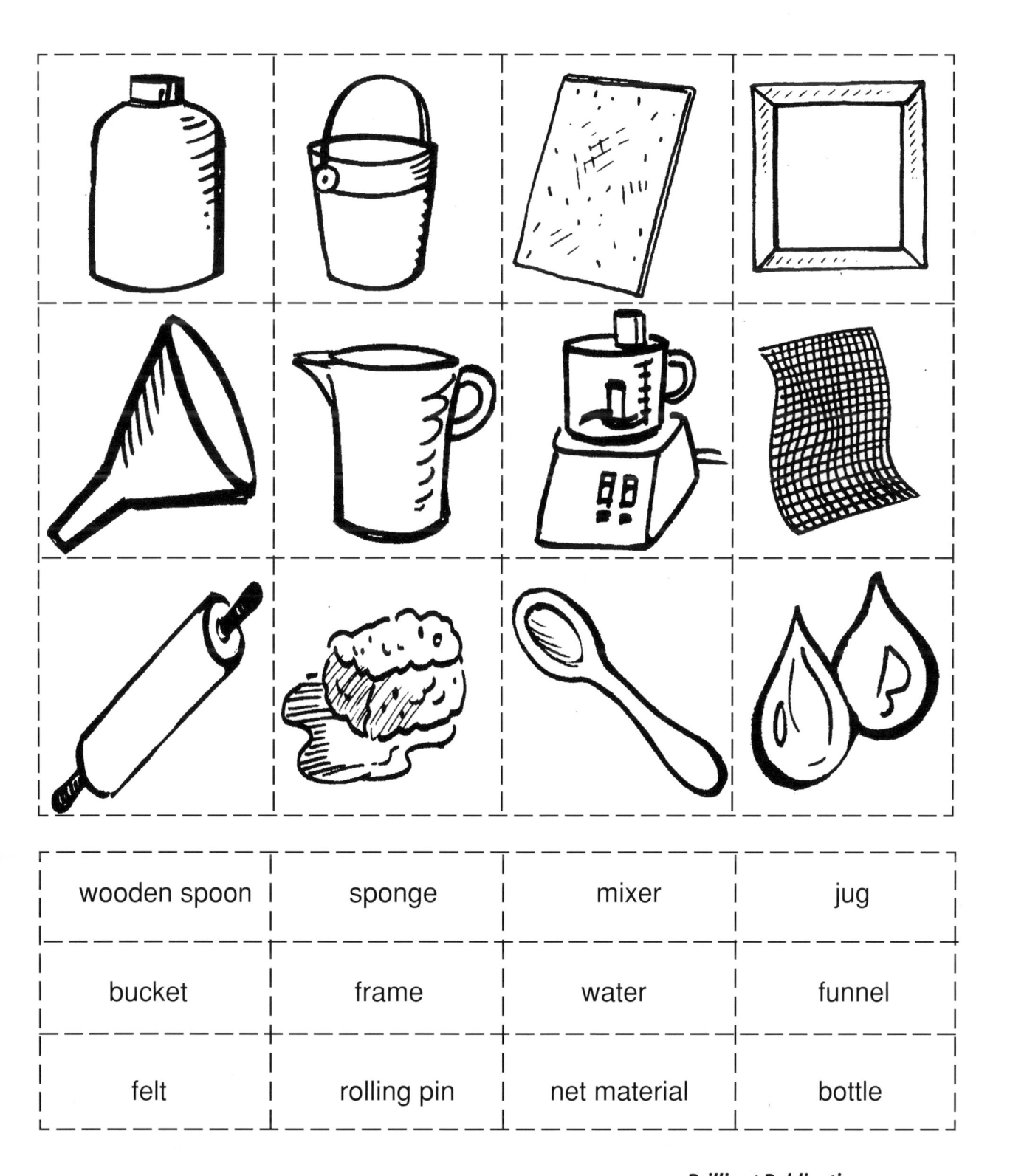

wooden spoon	sponge	mixer	jug
bucket	frame	water	funnel
felt	rolling pin	net material	bottle

© User Friendly Resource Enterprises Ltd.

Brilliant Publications
www.brilliantpublications.co.uk

45

Making paper

Paper making

There are many ways to make paper. The following is one simple process that could be used in the classroom.

Making the pulp

1. Paper can be made from tissues, computer paper or photocopy paper.
2. Tear the paper into small squares and soak at least overnight.
3. Put small handfuls of the soaked paper into a blender to separate the fibres. Don't mix too long.

If you don't want to use a blender you could pound the paper squares with a stick in a large bucket.

Making the paper

1. Put a piece of felt on top of a pile of newspapers. Make sure it is level. Put the frame on top of the felt.
2. Fill the jug with pulp. Pour the pulp inside the frame. Give the frame one quick shake left, right, up and down.
3. Mop up the water around outside of the frame with the sponge.
4. Remove the frame carefully and then put another piece of felt on to the paper.
5. Press the top felt down and mop up the excess water. Repeat the sponging, removing as much water as possible.
6. Roll the rolling pin over the top of the pile to expel the last of the water.
7. Peel off the top piece of felt carefully and hang up the piece of paper, still on the bottom felt, to dry.
8. Pour the excess pulp through some fine netting. Store in a sealed bottle or container.

Different types of paper

Paper making

Describe all the different types of paper below. Use some words from the list below to get you started.

Colourful
Thick
Strong
Soft
Thin

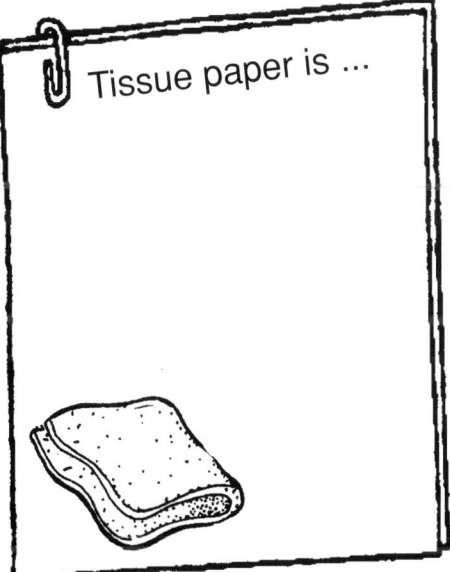

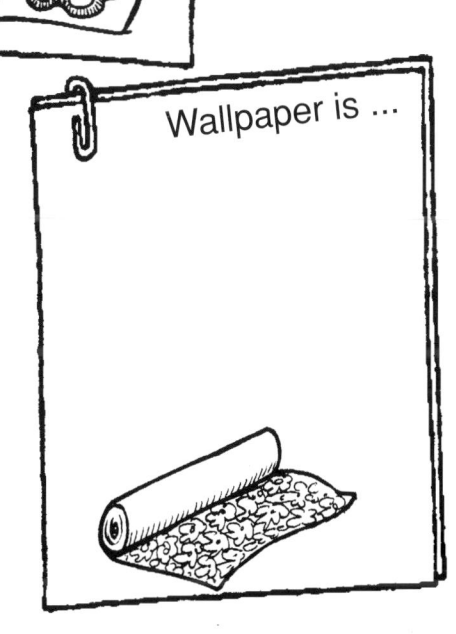

Wrapping paper is …

Cardboard is …

Art paper is …

Tissue paper is …

Wallpaper is …

© User Friendly Resource Enterprises Ltd.

Brilliant Publications
www.brilliantpublications.co.uk

Paper making

Colouring the paper

Here are three ways to colour the paper that you make.

Add some coloured pieces of paper to the paper pulp. Use lots of colours to create a mottled effect.

Add some powdered paint, ink or food-colouring to the pulp.

Paint the finished piece of paper.

Can you make some coloured paper?

Colour my T-shirt in the colour you are going to make.

This is the equipment I will need ...

This is the way I will colour my paper ...

48 Brilliant Publications
www.brilliantpublications.co.uk   © User Friendly Resource Enterprises Ltd.

Can you make paper?

Name _____

Paper making

| I can make paper ... | ☺ | 😐 | ☹ |

| I can make coloured paper ... | ☺ | 😐 | ☹ |

| Papermaking is easy ... | ☺ | 😐 | ☹ |

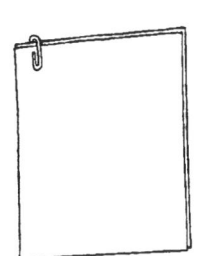

Can you think of a different way to make some interesting paper?

Integrating other curriculum areas

You've got mail!

Science
Materials
What makes stamps stick?

English
Letter Writing
Postcards

Mathematics
Geometry nets

Geography
Stamps from other cultures

Art and design
Postcard design
Stamp design

PSHE
Communicating feelings

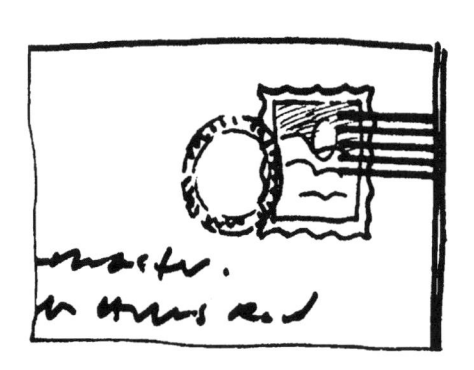

Project overview

You've got mail!

Letters and technology

A letter writing project is a popular and generally successful integrated project for 4–7 year olds. Each time I have used this project, children's writing skills have rapidly improved as they see a purpose for their writing, and they are usually writing with a genuine context and audience. This is also a very straightforward technology project as it can be completed without a lot of extra resources or equipment.

The project can be adapted for younger children by enlarging worksheets to A3 size and completing as a whole class activity.

The focus for this project is information and communication technology. Letter writing is a good basis to start with and then you can easily extend the project to include emails and fax communication.

Extension ideas

- Visit the local post office to observe the mail process.
- Write to pen-pals in other classes or in other schools.
- Design postcards.
- Write letters to put into a time capsule that can be opened at the end of the year.
- Investigate stamps from other cultures.
- Send (and receive!) mail to and from extra-terrestrials!

Assessment

Each of the activity sheets represents a learning objective outlined on the lesson sequence page. Photocopies of the completed template sheets can be used as samples for the purpose of portfolio assessment, or included in the cumulative files of each child.

You've got mail!

Suggested lesson sequence

Design brief
Let's see if we can design a system for sending post around our class.

Lesson 1: Setting the scene
Key question: How do we communicate using the postal system?
Learning objective: The pupils will sequence pictures to show the mail process.
Template: What happens when we post a letter?

Lesson 2: Developing background knowledge
Key question: How can we communicate using a letter?
Learning objective: The students will write a letter.
Template: Writing a letter

Lesson 3: Developing background knowledge
Key question: What are stamps and what are they for?
Learning objective: The pupils will investigate and design their own stamp.
Templates: Stamps
Design a stamp

Lesson 4: Considering the options
Key question: What can we use to wrap our letter?
Learning objective: The pupils will design an envelope for their letter.
Template: Envelopes

Lesson 5: Promoting our ideas
Key question: What rules will we need for using the post box?
Learning objective: The students will draw up a list of rules for distribution of the post.
Template: Classroom post

Lesson 6: Deciding on a solution
Key question: How can we distribute the post?
Learning objective: The children will design post boxes for collecting class post.
Template: Design a post box

Lesson 7: Evaluating our designs
Key question: Did I get a letter from our class postal system?
Learning objective: The pupils will reflect on the performance of the postal system.
Template: Testing our postal system

What happens when we post a letter?

Cut out the boxes and put them in order to show the post system.

You've got mail!

Pick up the letter from the mat.

The postman delivers the letter.

Write a letter.

Put the letter in the post box.

Read the letter and write back.

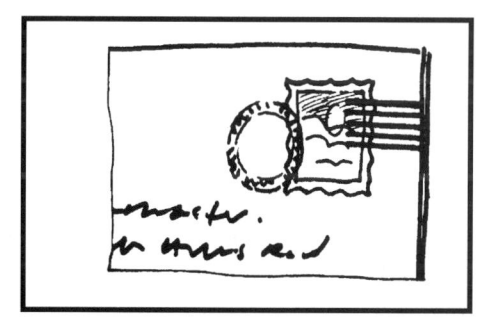

The post office sorts and franks the letter.

Put the letter in an envelope.

Put the address and stamp on the letter.

© User Friendly Resource Enterprises Ltd.

Brilliant Publications
www.brilliantpublications.co.uk

Writing a letter

You've got mail!

Talk about the parts of a letter in this diagram and then write your own letter below.

	24 Blue St Yellow Town	Your address
	Monday 21st September	The date
This is the person who the letters is for	Dear Ms Black	
	Thank you for your letter. I am having lots of fun painting colourful pictures. Please write back soon.	Write an interesting message
This is who wrote the letter	Yours sincerely Mrs Green	

Stamps

You've got mail!

We use stamps to pay for the cost of delivering our letters. Stamps cost different prices depending on how far the letters have to go. Some people collect stamps.

The cost of the stamp.
Letters cost less than parcels to post.

The picture.
Stamps have interesting pictures on them, sometimes of famous people or scenery.

THE STATION

Stick some used stamps here.

Post office workers frank letters as they sort the post. The franking tells us where and when a letter was sent.

You've got mail!

Design a stamp

Design some of your own stamps.
If you design a stamp for another country, remember to add on the name of the country. Don't forget to draw an interesting picture and write the cost on the stamp too.

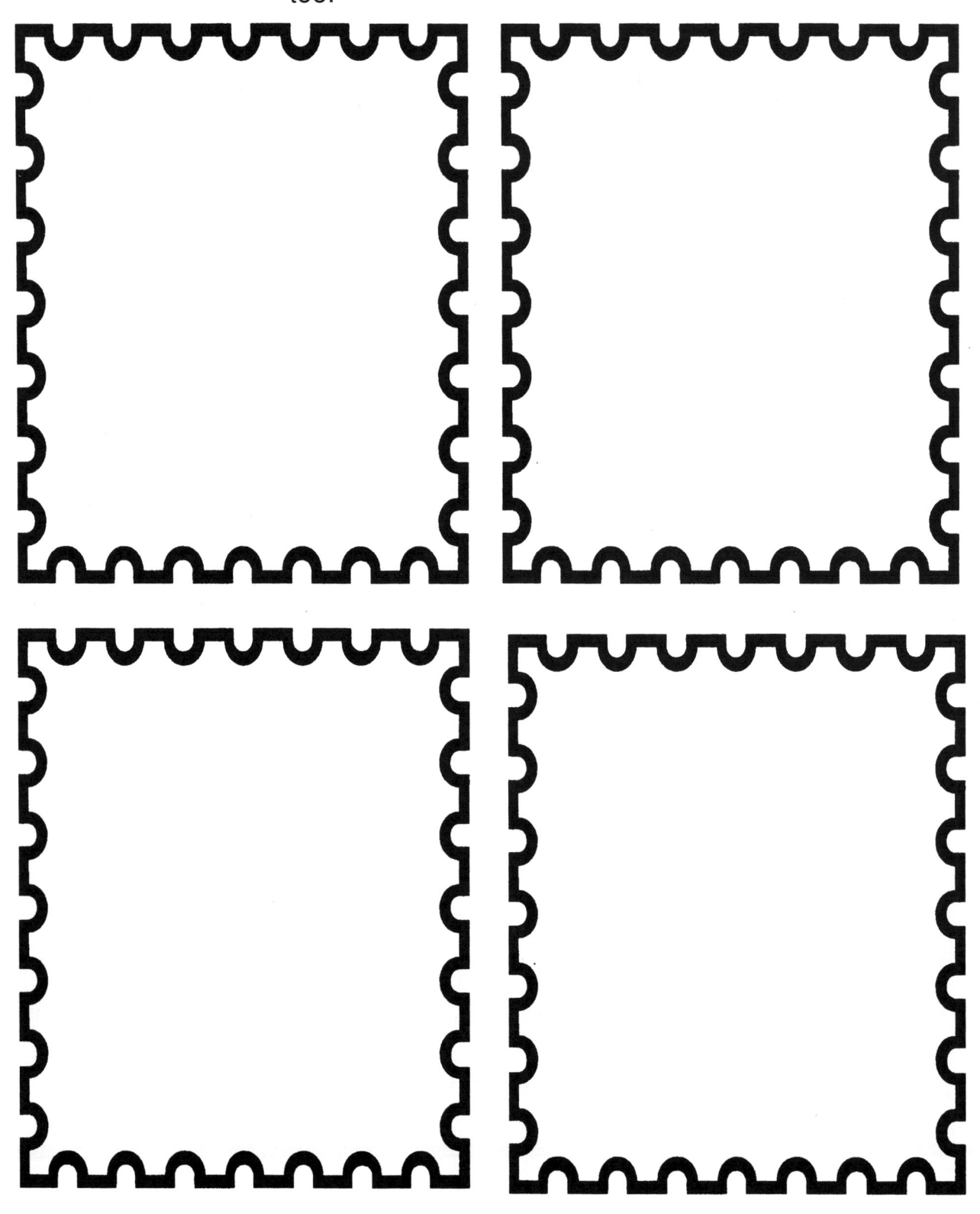

Envelopes

Let's make an envelope to put our letter in. It is easy to fold an envelope using a piece of square paper. Open up some different sized envelopes to see how they were folded.

You've got mail!

Here is a simple net that you could use for making an envelope.

Start with a piece of paper.

The flap

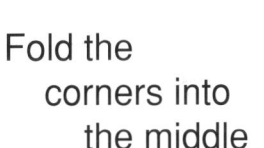

Fold the corners into the middle

Once you have made an envelope, have a go at changing your design.
- Can you make an envelope out of a *round* piece of paper?
- Can you make an envelope to fit your letter exactly?
- Can you design a new net?

Classroom post

You've got mail! Let's write some rules for sending letters around our class.

When will we write the letters?

Where will we put the post?

How will we give out the post?

How can we make sure that everyone gets a letter?

Design a post box

You've got mail!

Design a post box so that you can send letters to your classmates.

Draw your ideas, then choose your best one.

The materials I will need to make my post box are:

_____   _____
_____   _____
_____   _____
_____   _____

Testing our postal system

You've got mail!

Name _____

Can you write a letter?

Can you make an envelope?

Can you make a post box?

I enjoyed writing and receiving letters because ...

Integrating other curriculum areas

The picnic party

Science
Materials
Preserving food
Heating and cooling
Healthy eating

English
Writing menus
Invitations

Mathematics
Graphing

History/geography
How food was preserved
Eating outside

Art and design
Weaving picnic baskets

Physical education
Picnic games

PSHE
Risk management

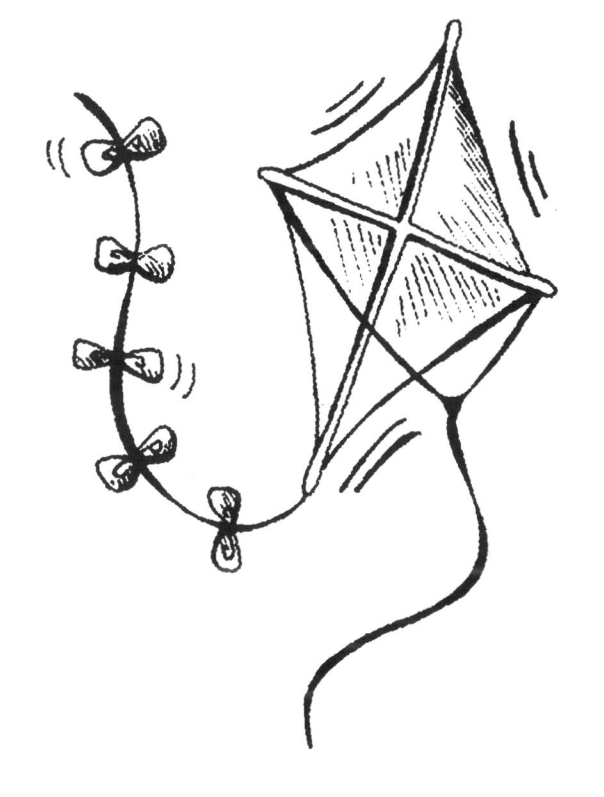

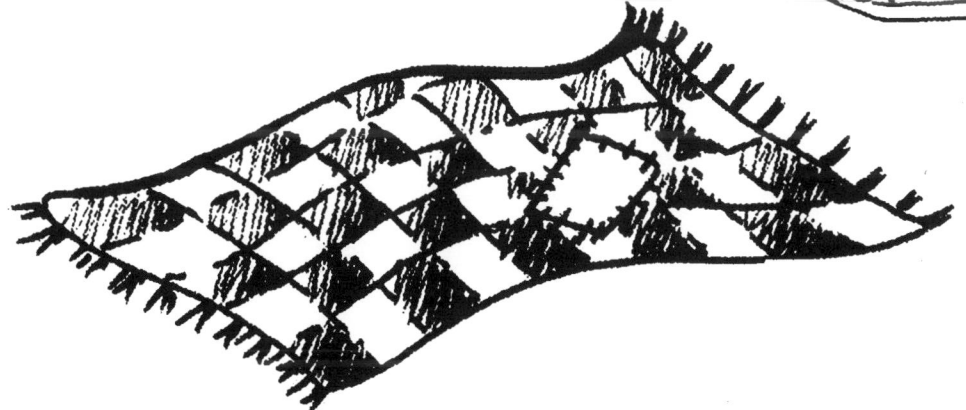

The picnic party

Project overview

Picnics and technology

Children are always interested in this project because it involves food! It links easily with health and physical education, and projects about healthy eating.

This project can be adapted for younger children by enlarging worksheets to A3 size and completing as a whole class activity.

The main focus for this project is food technology, incorporating the safe storage and packaging of foods. The project also includes materials technology, as children investigate the features of different food containers. There are opportunities in this project for the children to gather and graph data in a simple form.

Extension ideas

- Design a system to keep a drink cool.
- Design a basket to take to the picnic.
- Write a healthy picnic menu.
- Investigate and compare different picnic locations.
- Organise a teddy bear's picnic.

Assessment

Each of the activity sheets represents a learning objective outlined on the lesson sequence page. Photocopies of the completed template sheets can be used as samples for the purpose of portfolio assessment, or included in the cumulative files of each child.

Suggested lesson sequence

The picnic party

Design brief
We're going on a picnic party – but how will we store our sandwiches?

Lesson 1: Setting the scene
Key question: What do we take on picnics?
Learning objective: The pupils will identify the items that are commonly taken on a picnic.
Template: What will we take on our picnic?

Lesson 2: Developing background knowledge
Key question: What food will we take?
Learning objective: The pupils will survey the class and graph sandwich preferences.
Template: Graph of our favourite sandwiches

Lesson 3: Developing background knowledge
Key question: What would happen if we left food unprotected?
Learning objective: The pupils will investigate unprotected food to see what happens.
Template: What will happen to unprotected food?

Lesson 4: Considering the options
Key question: How are food containers different?
Learning objective: The pupils will complete a chart to describe the features of different food containers.
Template: How are food containers different?

Lesson 5: Deciding on a solution
Key question: What kind of container will we need?
Learning objective: The children will match foods with the features needed for protecting them.
Template: How do we store different foods?

Lesson 6: Constructing our designs
Key question: What will our picnic food containers look like?
Learning objective: The pupils will draw a plan of their containers.
Template: Designing our picnic containers

Lesson 7: Evaluating our designs
Key question: Did my container keep my picnic food in a good condition?
Learning objective: The pupils will reflect on the performance of their containers.
Template: Testing my container

The picnic party

What will we take on our picnic?

Circle the things you think are important to take on a picnic, then draw yourself on a picnic.

Name:

Tally chart
Record the data here.

Jam

Honey

Tomato

Ham

The picnic party
Date:

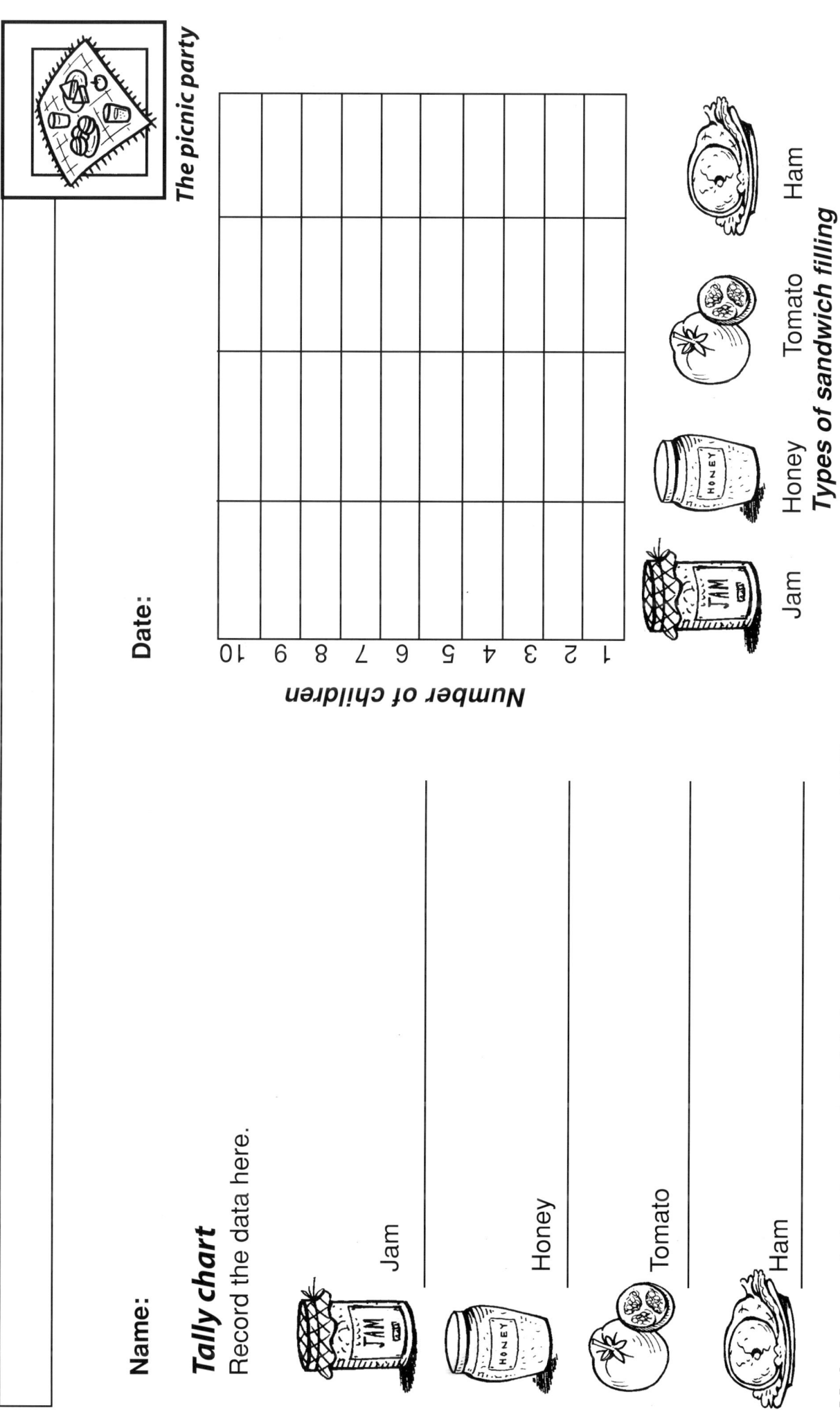

Number of children
1 2 3 4 5 6 7 8 9 10

Jam Honey Tomato Ham
Types of sandwich filling

Make a graph to show what drinks your class would like to have on a picnic.

© User Friendly Resource Enterprises Ltd.

Brilliant Publications
www.brilliantpublications.co.uk

65

What will happen to unprotected food?

The picnic party

What would happen if we took these unprotected foods on our picnic?

Tomatoes

Ham

Sandwiches

Eggs

Ice Cream

How are food containers different?

The picnic party

You need something to protect your food on a picnic!

Fill in the chart to show the features of each container. Write ✓ or ✗	Will the container keep the food cool?	Is the container airtight?	Is the container strong?	Is the container watertight?	Can the food container be recycled?	Draw some food that could be stored in this container.

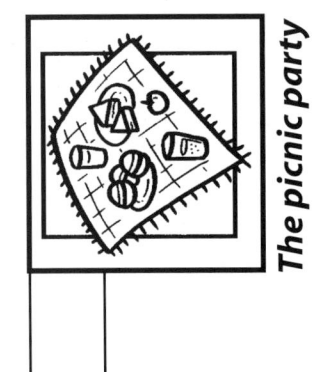

How do we store different foods?

The picnic party

Fill in the chart to show how to store each food below. Write 'yes', 'no' or 'I don't know'.	Does the food need to stay cool?	Will the food need to be in an airtight container?	Will the food need to be in a strong container?	Will the food need to be in a watertight container?	Draw a container that you could use to store each of these foods.

Brilliant Publications
www.brilliantpublications.co.uk

© User Friendly Resource Enterprises Ltd.

Designing our picnic containers

The picnic party

Your task is to design a container to take your sandwiches to the picnic, and protect them. Don't forget your container will need to be both *airtight* and *strong* so that your sandwiches stay fresh all the way to the picnic!

Draw your ideas in the plates. Choose your best design. Write the materials you need to make it inside the picnic basket.

The picnic party

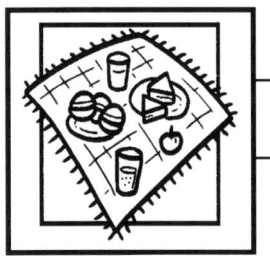

Testing my container

Name _____

Was the container strong?

☺ 😐 ☹

Was the container airtight?

☺ 😐 ☹

Did the container keep the sandwiches fresh?

☺ 😐 ☹

My sandwiches tasted ...

The best part of my container was ...

Integrating other curriculum areas

Let's go fly a kite!

Science
Wind
Seasons

English
Diagrams
Advertisements
Instructions

Mathematics
Symmetrical shapes
Measurements

Geography
Kites from other cultures

Art and design
Designs on kites
Moving like kites

Physical education
Kite games

PSHE
Co-operation
Safety

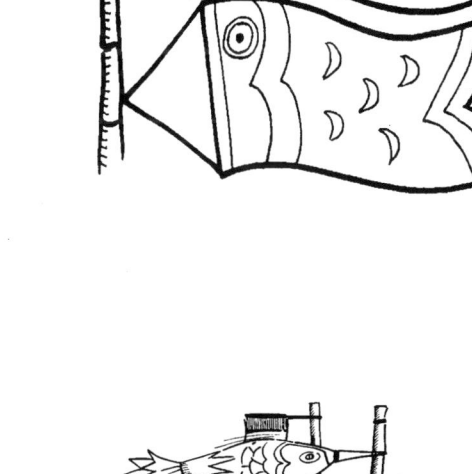

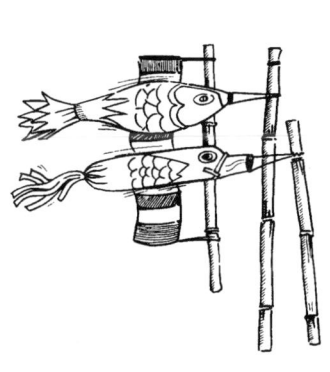

Project overview

Let's go fly a kite!

Kites and technology

Kites is a fabulous topic for capturing children's interest, especially when they can fly their creations. You may want to think about the time of year you use this project – you can't fly your kites without any wind!

The key focus points are: a kite must be balanced, a kite must be symmetrical and a kite should be stable. It is worth returning to these points throughout the project. Lessons in the project focusing on balance and symmetry are designed to reinforce these concepts.

In this project the children will focus on materials technology as they investigate the best materials to use for their kites. These activities also integrate well with science objectives.

Younger children will need support to make their kites successfully. Inviting parents to a kite-making workshop is a great idea. There also may be a specialist kite shop in your area that is willing to demonstrate the making and flying of kites. Sometimes kite shops also have simple kite kits that could be used in school.

This project can be adapted for younger children by enlarging worksheets to A3 size and completing as a whole class activity.

Extension ideas
- Investigate other flying things such as darts.
- Compete to see which kite flies the longest or which kite can hold the heaviest weight in the air.
- Talk about other ways people use wind such as windmills and gliders.
- Make a kite with two strings and try to make the kite 'do tricks' in the sky.
- Write stories about a runaway kite or what it would be like to fly on a kite.

Assessment

Each of the activity sheets represents a learning objective outlined on the lesson sequence page. Photocopies of the completed template sheets can be uses as samples for the purpose of portfolio assessment, or included in the cumulative files of each child.

Suggested lesson sequence

Let's go fly a kite!

Design brief
Our class is going to have a kite festival. Can you produce a kite that will fly?

Lesson 1: Setting the scene
Key question: What is a kite?
Learning objective: The pupils will identify the key parts of a kite.
Template: What is a kite?

Lesson 2: Developing background knowledge
Key question: What is a symmetrical shape?
Learning objective: The pupils will complete a symmetrical picture of a kite.
Template: What is symmetry?

Lesson 3: Developing background knowledge
Key question: How can we balance an object?
Learning objective: The pupils will make a parachute and then adapt their design to keep it in the air.
Template: Making a parachute

Lesson 4: Investigating other cultures
Key question: What is a Chinese kite?
Learning objective: The pupils will view some examples of kites from other cultures, and design a colourful Chinese kite, incorporating animals or flowers.
Template: Kites from other cultures

Lesson 5: Deciding on a solution
Key question: What material will help the kite to fly?
Learning objective: The pupils will investigate material for their kites.
Template: What material will be best for my kite?

Lesson 6: Constructing our designs
Key question: How can we make a kite?
Learning objective: The pupils will make a kite. Older pupils will select or draw their own pattern. Younger children will make adaptations to a standard pattern.
Template: Making our kites: teacher information

Lesson 7: Testing and evaluating our designs
Key questions: Did my kite fly? Where is it safe to fly our kite?
Learning objective: The pupils will design an advertisement for flying it safely. The pupils will evaluate their kite designs.
Templates: Testing my kite
Flying our kites

Key focus points:
A kite must be balanced
A kite must be symmetrical
A kite should be stable

What is a kite?

Let's go fly a kite!

Label the parts of the kite from the list below.

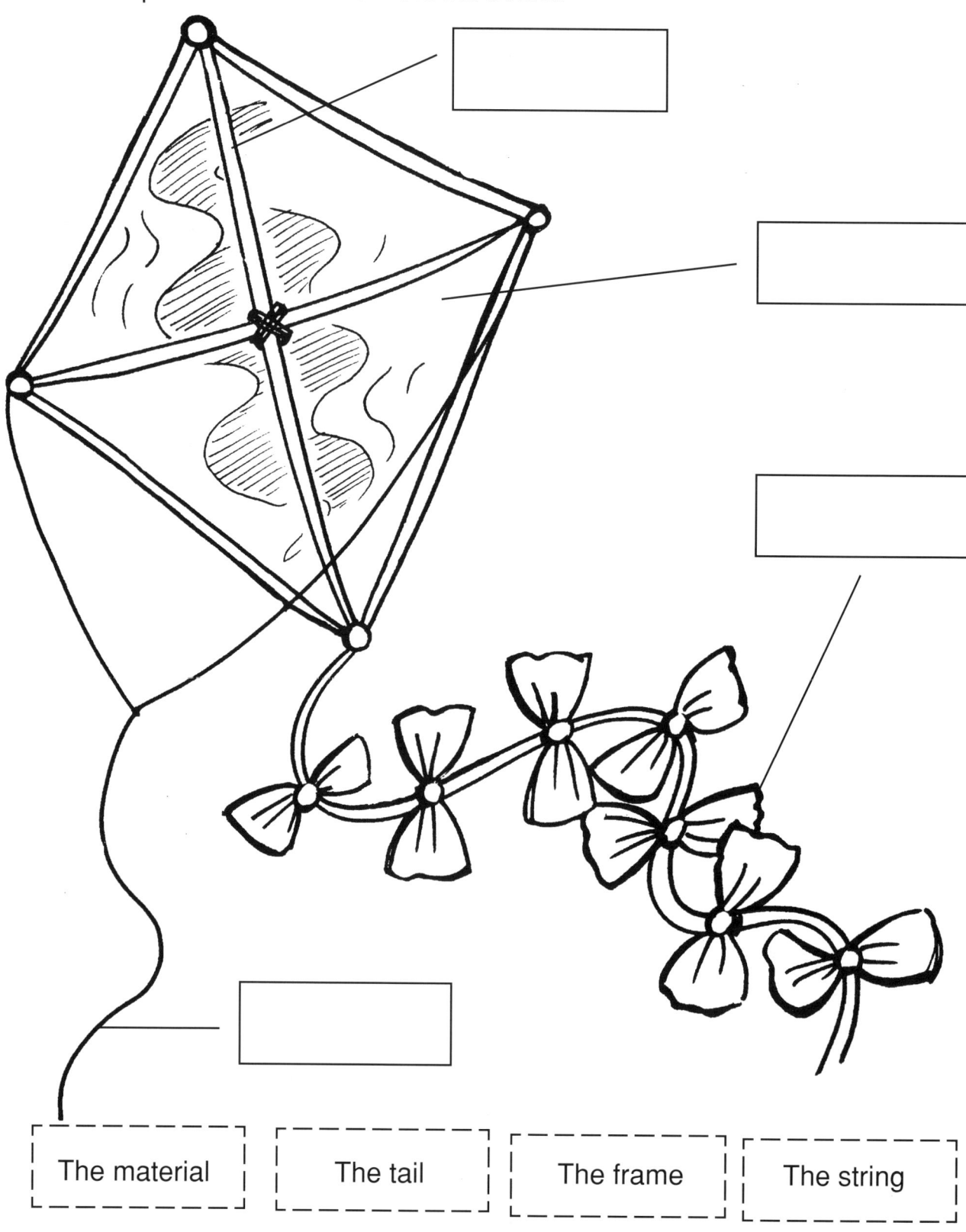

| The material | The tail | The frame | The string |

What is symmetry?

Let's go fly a kite!

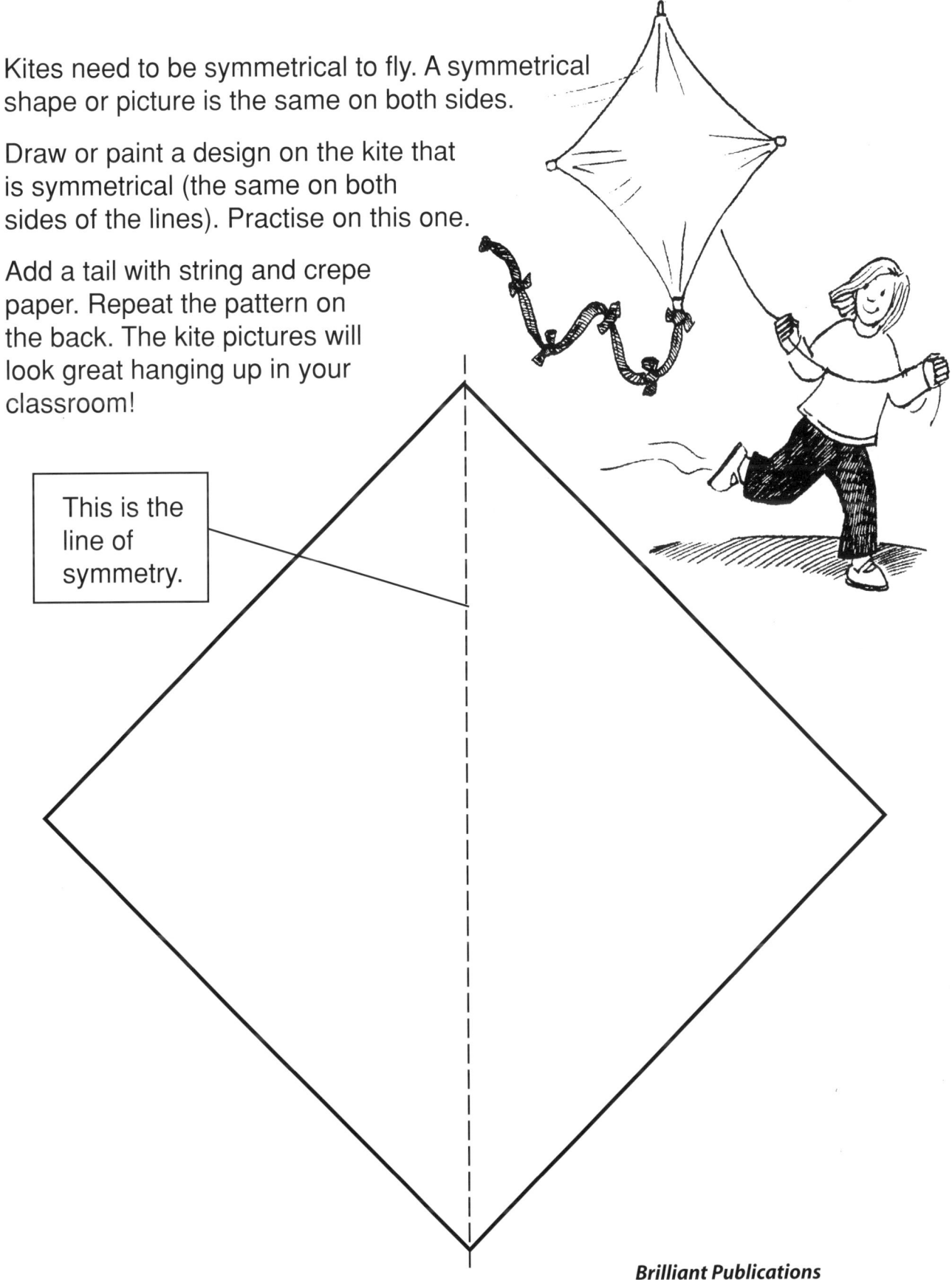

Kites need to be symmetrical to fly. A symmetrical shape or picture is the same on both sides.

Draw or paint a design on the kite that is symmetrical (the same on both sides of the lines). Practise on this one.

Add a tail with string and crepe paper. Repeat the pattern on the back. The kite pictures will look great hanging up in your classroom!

This is the line of symmetry.

Making a parachute

Let's go fly a kite!

Kites need to be balanced to fly. Parachutes also need to be balanced to work.

Let's practise getting the balance right by making a parachute.

You need:
scissors; Plasticine®; string; plastic

1. Cut the plastic into a square.
2. Tie a piece of string to each corner.
3. Join the string ends together with the Plasticine®.
4. Watch your parachute drift to the ground.

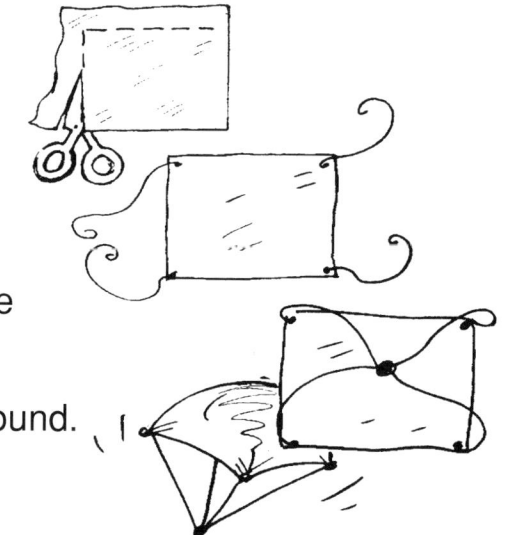

- Time your parachute.

- How can you make it better?

- Think about material, balance and weight.

Kites from other cultures

Let's go fly a kite!

Kites are an important part of the Chinese culture. It takes many years to become a master kite maker. Chinese people often fly their kites during festivals.

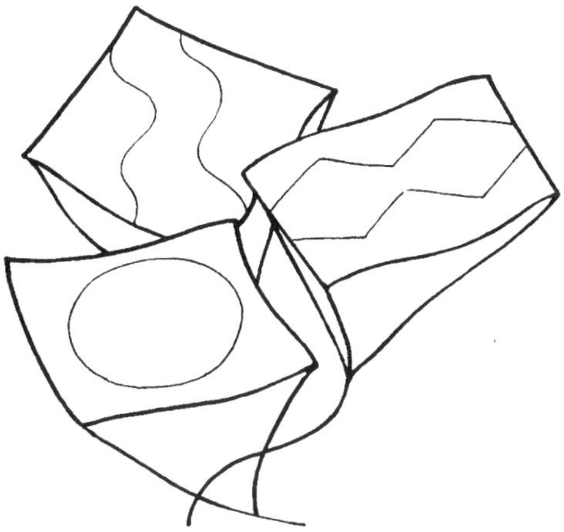

They make beautiful kites to fly and they often attach small lanterns to the kites.

Sometimes the owners try to knock each other's kites out of the air!

The Chinese kites are often quite complicated to make, and turn into lovely butterflies, birds, flowers and animals.

Design your own kite in the box below. Include lots of bright colours in your picture to make your kite look interesting. Remember whatever shape you choose, it needs to be symmetrical!

Let's go fly a kite!

What material will be best for my kite?

Put these material features in order of importance from number 1–4. Number 1 is the most important feature of kite material.

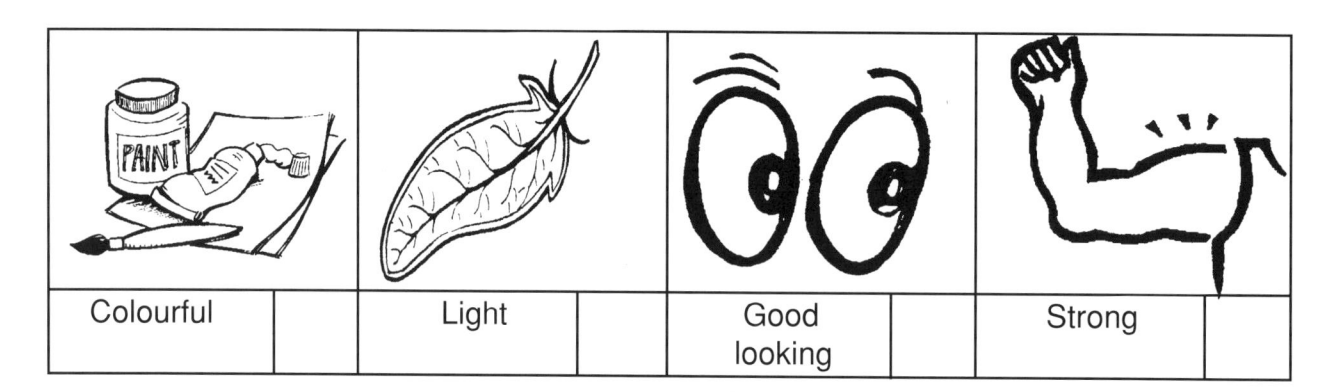

Colourful		Light		Good looking		Strong	

Cut up some small scraps of material that you think you could use for a kite. Paste the material inside the kite shape here. If they don't all fit glue other pieces around the kite.

Brilliant Publications
www.brilliantpublications.co.uk

© User Friendly Resource Enterprises Ltd.

Making our kites: teacher information

Let's go fly a kite!

There are lots of different kinds of kites that you can easily make with children, especially with a bit of extra parent help. These are some basic ideas but lots of others can be found on the Internet.

Many cities also have a specialist kite shop that may run workshops. Advertise for kite enthusiasts to come and demonstrate their kites.

The plastic bag kite

You will need:
plastic supermarket bags
kebab sticks
string
sticky tape
stickers to decorate

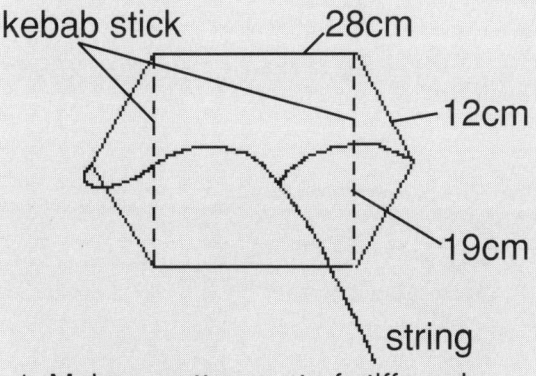

kebab stick — 28cm — 12cm — 19cm — string

1. Make a pattern out of stiff card.
2. Trace the shape onto a flat supermarket bag.
3. Cut out the shape and tape on the kebab sticks. Make sure they are taped at the top and bottom to stop them from slipping out.
4. Decorate your kite.
5. Attach the string to the side points.
6. Find the middle of this piece of string and attach the long string to fly your kite.

The diamond kite

You will need:
2 beams of straw, bamboo, willow or dowel
string
plastic or cellophane
paper

1. Tie together 2 beams to form a cross. You could use straws, bamboo, willow or dowel depending on how heavy your kite is going to be.

2. Tie a piece of string around the edge of the cross and secure. Notches on the ends of the cross will help to keep the string in place.

3. Attach material to the kite. Plastic or cellophane would work well.

4. Make the tail from a piece of string. Tie some pieces of paper on to the string.

5. Tie a string on to the top and bottom. Attach a long string to this. Remember the string has to be strong and that wire is unsafe to use.

© User Friendly Resource Enterprises Ltd.

Brilliant Publications
www.brilliantpublications.co.uk

Flying our kites

Let's go fly a kite!

Use the pictures and rules below to make an advertisement for flying kites safely. Don't forget to make your advertisement bright and interesting.

Don't fly close to houses!

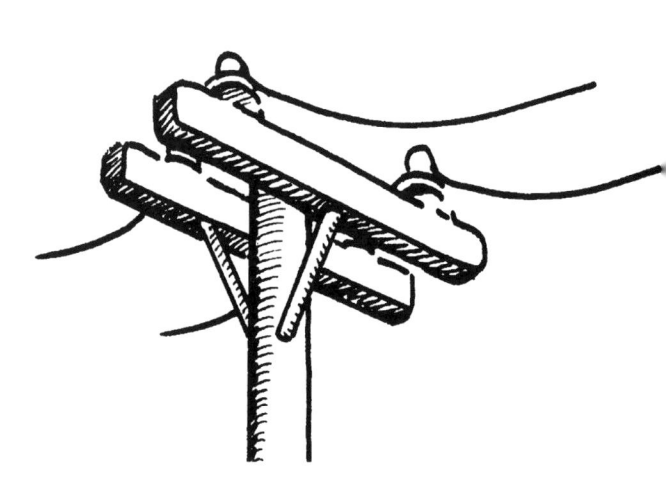

Don't fly close to power lines!

Don't fly kites close to trees!

Watch out for rope burn!

Brilliant Publications
www.brilliantpublications.co.uk

© User Friendly Resource Enterprises Ltd.

Testing my kite

Let's go fly a kite!

Name _____

| Is my kite strong? | 😊 | 😐 | ☹️ |

| Is my kite symmetrical? | 😊 | 😐 | ☹️ |

| Is my kite balanced? | 😊 | 😐 | ☹️ |

| Did my kite fly? Why... | 😊 | 😐 | ☹️ |

Teddy chairs

Integrating other curriculum areas

Teddy chairs

Science
Construction materials
Weight

English
Describing chairs
Complaints about chairs

Mathematics
Measurement

History
Chairs throughout history

Art and design
Designs
Miming different chairs

PSHE
Safety

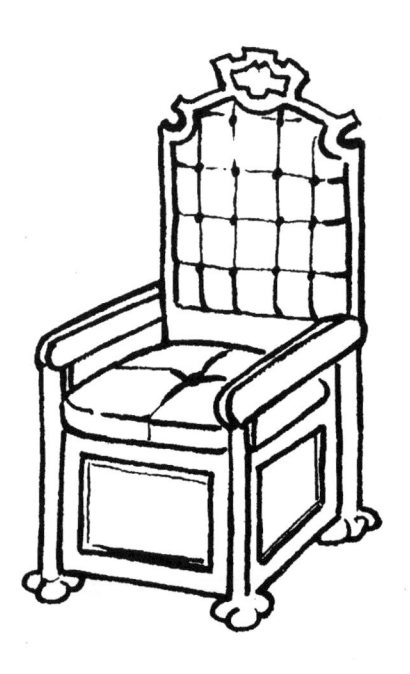

Project overview

Chairs and technology
Teddy chairs

Chairs are great for study as there are so many handy and practical examples for the children to investigate. The distinguishing features are easy for the children to see and account for.

This project can be adapted for younger children by enlarging templates to A3 size and completing as a whole class activity.

In this project the focus is structure and mechanisms, as the children investigate the way chairs are structured to meet certain needs.

A lesson for making a paper tower is included in the project to give the children the background knowledge they will need to build paper structures. This lesson could be repeated to give children opportunities to practise what they have learnt. The children may need to be taught how to roll the paper to give it strength and how to join the paper together.

Extension ideas
- Investigate the ergonomics of chairs.
- Conduct a class survey to find out which are the most comfortable chairs.
- Design a chair of the future.
- Plan and make a table to go with teddy's chair.
- Design some chairs for use in a classroom.
- Design some chairs for use in the library.

Assessment
Each of the activity sheets represents a learning objective outlined on the lesson sequence page. Photocopies of the completed template sheets can be used as samples for the purpose of portfolio assessment, or included in the cumulative files of each child.

Suggested lesson sequence

Teddy chairs

> **Design brief**
> Have you ever wondered what a Teddy chair might look like? See if you can make one!

Lesson 1: Setting the scene
Key question: How are chairs different?
Learning objective: The pupils will complete a chart, matching people and chairs, that shows some of the varied uses for chairs.
Template: Chairs and people

Lesson 2: Developing background knowledge
Key question: How can we make paper strong?
Learning objective: The children will complete a mini-technology challenge to gain background knowledge that they will need later in the project.
Template: Making a tower

Lesson 3: Considering the options
Key question: What makes a chair strong?
Learning objective: The pupils will identify the design features of chairs and apply these to their own model.
Template: What makes a chair strong?

Lesson 4: Considering the options
Key question: What makes a chair safe?
Learning objective: The pupils will identify the design features of chairs and apply these to their own model.
Template: What makes a chair safe?

Lesson 5: Investigating the past
Key question: How are modern chairs different from those used in the past?
Learning objective: The pupils will group pictures of chairs as old or modern. The pupils will describe their groups.
Template: How have chairs changed?

Lesson 6: Constructing our designs
Key questions: What will our teddy chair look like? What's special about a chair for a teddy?
Learning objective: The children will draw their plans.
Template: Making our designs

Lesson 7: Evaluating our designs
Key question: Did the chair hold teddy?
Learning objective: The pupils will reflect on the performance of their chair.
Template: Testing my teddy chair

Chairs and people

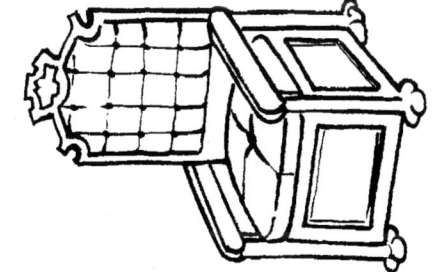

Match the chairs with the people who would be most likely to use them.

Teddy chairs

Brilliant Publications
www.brilliantpublications.co.uk

© User Friendly Resource Enterprises Ltd.

85

Teddy chairs

Making a tower

Let's practise our planning and building skills by making a paper tower.

The Challenge
Can you build a tower that can hold a cup?
You may use:
6 pieces of paper
sticky tape

Think carefully...
How can you make the paper strong?
How can you balance the tower?

My tower plan...

Did the tower work?

Next time I would...

Brilliant Publications
www.brilliantpublications.co.uk

© User Friendly Resource Enterprises Ltd.

86

What makes a chair strong?

Teddy chairs

Colour the parts of these chairs that make them extra strong. Now draw a picture of the strongest chair that you can think of.

The strongest chair I can think of

Now share your design with a friend. Can you think of any ways to improve your design?

What makes a make chair safe?

Teddy chairs

Colour the parts of these chairs that make them safe.
Now draw a picture of the safest chair that you can think of.

The safest chair I can think of

Now share your design with a friend. Can you think of any ways to improve your design?

Brilliant Publications
www.brilliantpublications.co.uk
© User Friendly Resource Enterprises Ltd.

How have chairs changed?

Teddy chairs

	Old	Modern
Cut out the chairs to paste on the chart.		
Describe the chairs.	The old chairs are...	The modern chairs are...

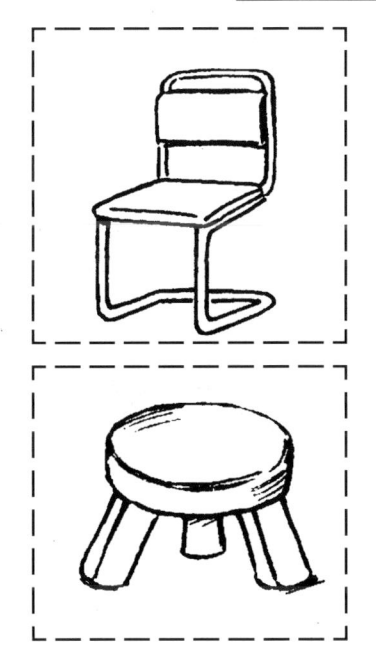

Teddy chairs

Making our designs

Your task

Your job is to design and build a chair for a teddy. The chair will need to be strong to hold teddy's weight and it will need to be safe so that teddy doesn't fall out.

Check what your teacher wants you to use:

paper	glue	sticky tape
card	boxes	ice block sticks

Draw your plans before you begin!

Colour the pictures to show the features of the chairs.
Is it going to be strong?
Is it going to be comfortable?
Does it look good?
What makes it special for teddy?
Where would teddy use it?

Testing my teddy chair

Teddy chairs

Name _____

Is my chair strong?

☺ 😐 ☹

Is my chair safe?

☺ 😐 ☹

Did my chair hold teddy?

☺ 😐 ☹

Next time I could...